BRITISH RAIL FLEET SURVEY

11 Overhead Line Electric Multiple~Units

BRITISH RAIL FLEET SURVEY

11 Overhead Line Electric Multiple~Units

Alec Swain

LONDON
IAN ALLAN LTD

Contents

First published 1990

ISBN 0 7110 1902 9

Published by Ian Allan Ltd, Shepperton, Surrey;
and printed by Ian Allan Printing Ltd at their works
at Coombelands in Runnymede, England

Front cover:
**This view taken at Billericay on 11 July 1989
shows unit No 321310 working the 14.04
Liverpool Street-Southend Victoria service.**
Alec Swain

Back cover:
**Class 306 unit No 017 was retained at Ilford
depot following withdrawal of other
members of the class and is now used on
special workings. It now carries BR multiple-
unit green livery albeit with yellow warning
panels.** *Brian Morrison*

Half title:
**Class 321 unit No 321308 approaches
Hinxton Crossing with the 12.05 Liverpool
Street-Cambridge service on 18 January
1989.** *John C. Baker*

Previous page:
**Class 317/1 unit No 317330 enters
Cricklewood station with the 11.28 Luton-
Moorgate service on 15 February 1988.**
David Brown

Below:
**Longsight stabling point on 16 June 1984
with representatives of Classes 303 and 304
completing the line-up.** *Les Nixon*

Introduction

In Part 6 of this series Brian Haresnape traced the history of the electric locomotive and the various options of power supply and means of current collection which are, of course, directly related to the introduction of the electric multiple-unit (EMU) train to this country. Subsequently Part 10 dealt specifically with those EMU trains which collect their traction current from a third rail, ie an addition to the two running rails, and at the same time dealt with the question of liveries carried over the years and other matters which are equally applicable to all EMU trains. Therefore I do not intend to go over the same ground in this, the eleventh in the *British Rail Fleet Survey* series, which will examine those EMU trains which utilise an overhead wire or, technically, a line for the collection of traction current.

As EMU classes became more numerous a system of classification became necessary and a series of numbers in the 'AM' (ac multiple-unit) series were allocated to each build, and ranged from 'AM2' to 'AM11' — these subsequently became Classes 302 to 311 under the later TOPS classification:

'AM2' — Class 302   'AM7' — Class 307
'AM3' — Class 303   'AM8' — Class 308
'AM4' — Class 304   'AM9' — Class 309
'AM5' — Class 305   'AM10' — Class 310
'AM6' — Class 306   'AM11' — Class 311

It is presumed that the classification AM1 was allocated to the Lancaster-Morecambe ac units.

There was a similar series AL1-AL5 for locomotives (AL — ac locomotives) as dealt with in Part 6. These locomotives became Classes 81-85.

On the question of vehicle classification codes I have used those gleaned from official BR publications which, I am the first to admit, do not always agree with those actually applied to the vehicle ends! The present-day term 'standard class' has also been applied for the sake of continuity, although some of the trains to be dealt with carried third class passengers in their earlier days — let alone second class.

Overhead Line EMU vehicle classification codes	
BDTBS	— Battery driving trailer brake standard
BDTC	— Battery driving trailer composite
BDTS	— Battery driving trailer standard
DMBS	— Driving motor brake standard
DMS	— Driving motor standard
DTBS	— Driving trailer brake standard
DTC	— Driving trailer composite
DTLV	— Driving trailer luggage van
DTS	— Driving trailer standard
MBS	— Motor brake standard
MLV	— Motor luggage van
MS	— Motor standard
PMS	— Pantograph motor standard
TC	— Trailer composite
TS	— Trailer standard

As with the third rail classes, there has been a certain amount of unit reformation and renumbering in recent years, often as the result of accident damage or reductions in unit length, eg the LMR Class 304 units. Such alterations are recorded monthly in the Ian Allan periodicals *Modern Railways* and *Motive Power Monthly* which update the Ian Allan *abc* volumes published each year. A useful reference work is *Motive Power Recognition: 2 Electric Multiple-Units* by Colin Marsden, published by Ian Allan Ltd and now in its second edition. Readers seeking a comprehensive history of the invention and evolution of the motive power, rolling stock and infrastructure which together comprise the electrified lines of today will find this in *The Age of the Electric Train* by J. C. Gillham, also published by Ian Allan Ltd. I am most grateful to the Secretary of The Electric Railway Society for permission to reproduce the drawings of the LYR Holcombe Brook stock, which first appeared in their long out-of-print monograph *The Electric Lines of the Lancashire & Yorkshire Railway*. My quest for information on this stock took me to GEC Transportation Projects Ltd at Trafford Park, one of the successors to Dick Kerr, and I must thank Mike Scott, Publicity Manager, for arranging access to the surviving archive material.

Finally I would like to thank Ian Allan Library, Colin Marsden, Ron Herbert, John Edgington, Jim Davenport, Bernard Harding, Murdoch Currie and many former railway colleagues for their assistance in locating suitable illustrations and providing information.

Alec Swain
Wembley, London 1989

The Genesis of the Overhead Line EMU

The principle of collecting traction current from an overhead line was first established in 1893 on the Isle of Man, by the Douglas & Laxey Coast Electric Tramway Ltd, under the direction of Dr Edward Hopkinson — a pioneer of electric rail traction. The first section of this 3ft gauge line was opened in September of that year, utilising a 500V supply, and eventually some 18 miles of line connected Derby Castle, Laxey and Ramsey. In March 1894 the company became The Isle of Man Tramways & Electric Power Co Ltd and then, in August 1902, the Manx Electric Railway Co Ltd. The first nine motor cars, equipped by Mather & Platt of Manchester, were originally provided with bow collectors, but these were replaced by tramway-type trolley poles in August 1898. The rolling stock eventually included 30 motor cars and 29 trailer cars, with the electrical equipment being supplied by a variety of manufacturers, and provided a choice of enclosed saloon or open seating.

The Snaefell Mountain Railway from Laxey to Snaefell Summit was opened by the same company in August 1895, and the single motor cars, with four Mather & Platt 25hp traction motors and closed saloon-type seating, collected their overhead line 550V supply via twin bow collectors. This was the highest voltage in use anywhere in the world at that time. Despite a gradient of 1 in 12 for much of its length, the line was worked by adhesion, the centre third rail being used for guidance and for braking under the Fell system. This required the 4½ miles or so of track to be laid to 3ft 6in gauge, as opposed to the 3ft gauge of the parent system.

Both lines remain in use to this day, although under the control of the Isle of Man Government since June 1957, and with much of the original equipment still in service they provide a unique opportunity to examine the work of the early designers and manufacturers of electric traction equipment.

The first of the pre-Grouping railways both to recognise the value of a higher voltage and lower current, which demanded fewer electrical sub-stations to maintain the line current and therefore less capital outlay, and introduce this form of traction, was the Midland Railway. Since a railway-owned power station already existed to supply Heysham Docks it was a simple matter to equip this to provide a 6,600V, 25 cycles, single phase ac supply for traction current when it was decided to

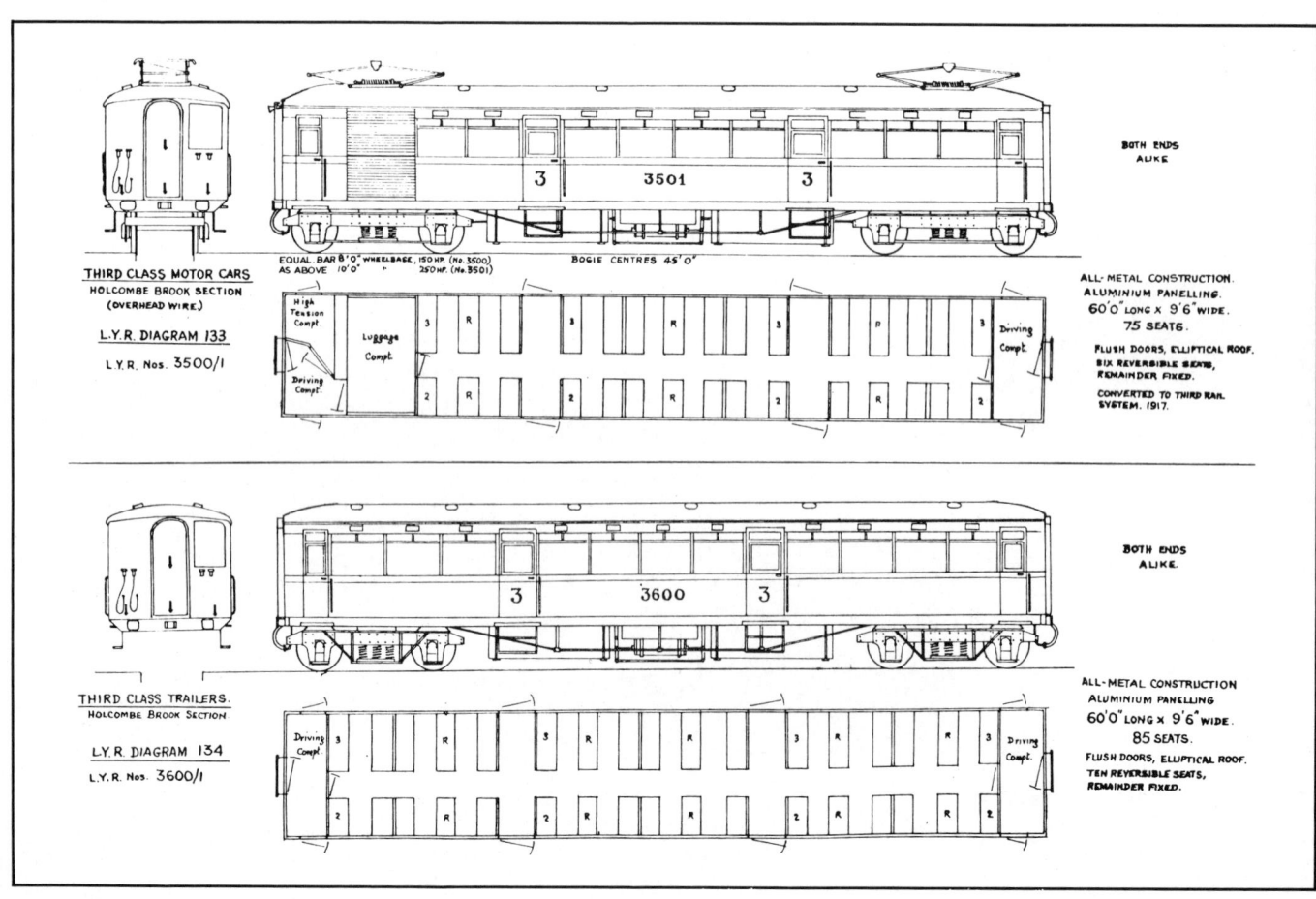

electrify the Lancaster to Morecambe/ Heysham lines, comprising some 18½ track miles. To work these lines the railway built seven new vehicles at their Derby works, of which three were 60ft motor cars and four were 43ft control trailers. The line provided the facility to try the products and systems of two manufacturers, a role it was to assume again at a much later date as it happened!

Two of the motor cars had Siemens 180hp traction motors with electro-magnetic control equipment and bow collectors, whilst the third had Westinghouse 150hp motors, electro-pneumatic control and a pantograph for current collection. The bow collectors were raised by vacuum motors fed from the train's vacuum brake system whilst the pantograph, on the Westinghouse-equipped motor car, was raised by an air motor — the system that is used today on BR. The motor cars were able to work singly or coupled to one or two trailer cars and,

Left:
Another view of motor coach No 28610, stabled at Morecambe Promenade, showing the other end of the vehicle. One of the 43ft control trailer coaches is alongside, and on the vehicle end can be seen the rudimentary fall plate which allowed staff to pass from vehicle to vehicle using the end doors. The different roof profile identifies it although the plate above the right-hand window can clearly be read — 18 tons 43'-0"×9'-0" — as final confirmation!
W. Hubert Foster/Ian Allan Library

Below left:
An excellent view of control trailer No 29292 in LMSR days. This coach seated no less than 56 persons within its 43ft length, and was well provided with guard irons on the bogies to deal with light obstructions on the track.
W. Hubert Foster/Ian Allan Library

for evaluation purposes and these three units in turn replaced the steam trains in August 1953. The remaining train was converted in 1956 using underslung Metropolitan-Vickers equipment as an alternative to the EE equipment which was carried within the motor coach. All four units continued to work the service until the whole system was abandoned in January 1966 and it is surely ironic that Lancaster Castle station, having hosted electric trains as early as 1908, was then to wait until March 1974 before seeing another!

At the same time the London Brighton & South Coast Railway was busy electrifying its South London suburban routes utilising a 6,700V ac overhead system and, although this was authorised and planned well before the Midland Railway scheme, that system opened in April 1908, whereas the Victoria to London Bridge service did not commence until December 1909. Eight 3-car trains were built by the Metropolitan Amalgamated Carriage & Wagon Co Ltd and comprised a first class trailer coach flanked by third class motor coaches, each of which had four Winter-Eichberg 115hp motors. Subsequent extensions required a further 34 motor and control trailer coaches from the Metropolitan Carriage & Wagon Co Ltd of Saltley, together with 36 similar control trailers from the Lancing works of the LBSCR. The extensions to Coulsdon North and Sutton by the Southern Railway in 1923-25 were really the completion of schemes drawn up much earlier and only delayed by World War 1,

despite the different control systems, all vehicles could be operated in multiple. Electric services were gradually introduced from April to September 1908, and the trains remained in service until 1951 when they were judged to be life-expired and were replaced by steam trains! The motor coaches and the two remaining control trailers were dismantled at Horwich works and, in view of their historical importance, it is a pity that none was set aside for preservation.

However, the line was destined to become a proving ground yet again and was converted to a 6,600V 50 cycles system that was to be adopted for the proposed electrification of the West Coast main line (WCML). Most of the distinctive portal-type masts were retained although the opportunity was taken to erect a number of different support systems for the overhead line to prove their suitability.

To operate the service it was decided to convert three of the four trains built by the Metropolitan Carriage Wagon & Finance Co Ltd at Saltley, Birmingham, for the 1914 London & North Western Railway service from Willesden Junction to Earls Court. These were three-car 630V dc third/fourth rail units incompatible with the later dc units operating the Euston/Broad Street to Watford, and North London line services and which had been in store since 1940 when the war put an end to the Earls Court service. To suit them for their new role their original Siemens equipment was removed and replaced by English Electric (EE) transformers, rectifiers and 215hp dc traction motors. Traction current was taken by either a pantograph or a Faiveley collector fitted to the roof just behind the driving compartment of the motor coach. One motor coach was equipped with a germanium rectifier

Above right:
Motor coach No M28222M, rebuilt from the 1914 LNWR Earls Court stock, stands at Morecambe in early BR days wearing the then standard green livery. Note that at this time it was not the practice to apply the vehicle number to the leading end. *GEC*

Right:
Driving trailer No M29023M heads the 12.40 Morecambe Promenade-Lancaster Castle service at Scale Hall station on 23 September 1964. This was a new station, opened in June 1957, and this stretch of the line was used to test various structures and catenary that would later appear in connection with the electrification of the West Coast main line.
Ron Herbert

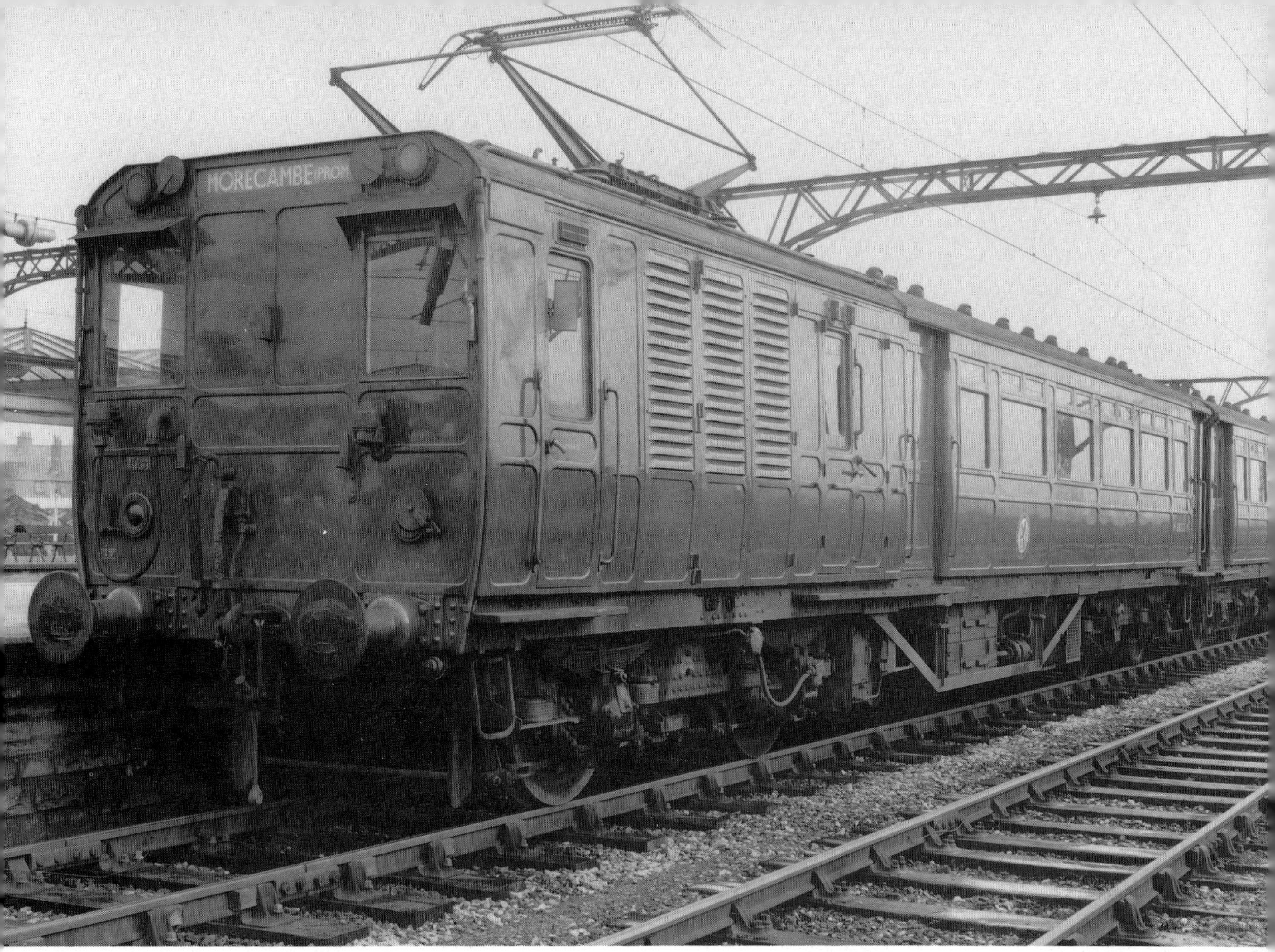
MORECAMBE (PROM

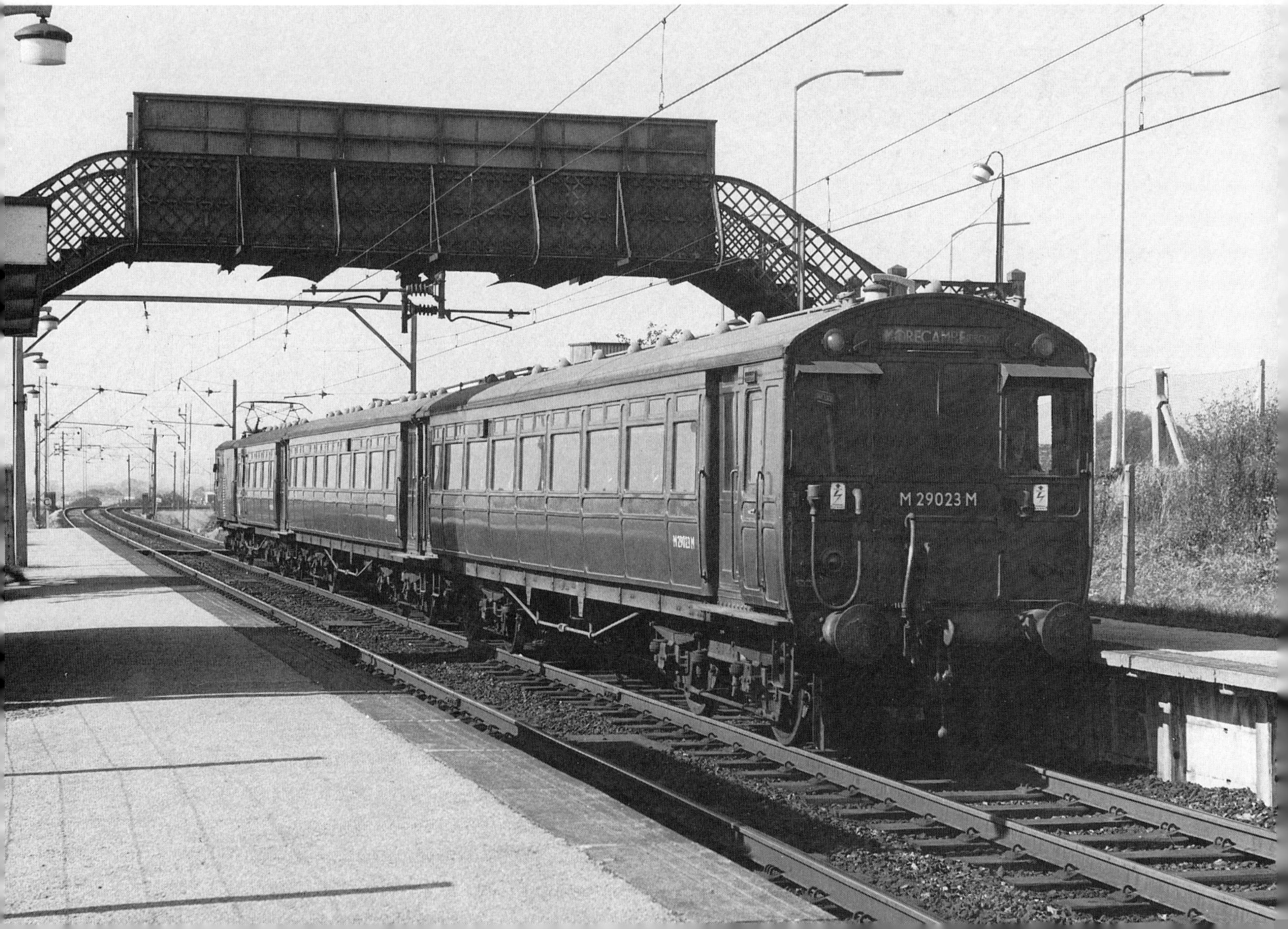
MORECAMBE PROM
M 29023 M

Left:
Motor coach No M28219M at Morecambe Promenade, showing a different bodyside arrangement just behind the driving compartment — evidently a more extensive rebuilding was necessary on this vehicle.
P. J. Sharpe

Below left:
London Brighton & South Coast Railway third class motor coach No 3260 for the Crystal Palace services, equipped with four 150hp Winter-Eichberg traction motors. Formed into three-car units together with control trailer coaches, two bow collectors were provided and were raised accordingly to suit the direction of travel.   *O. J. Morris/Ian Allan Library*

Below:
The first Southern Railway motor luggage van, No 10101, poses for the traditional official photograph at the Saltley works of its builder, the Metropolitan Carriage Wagon & Finance Co Ltd. Each axle had a 250hp GEC traction motor, and twin bow collectors were provided, these being raised by air pressure for the required direction of travel. When the Sutton and Coulsdon North services ceased in 1929, all 21 MLVs were stored for some years before conversion to bogie brake vans, this particular example then being numbered 56272. *GEC*

ran on 22 September 1929. The area south of the Thames remains dedicated to the third rail to this day.

The Lancashire & Yorkshire Railway had successfully introduced its 650V dc third rail system in the Liverpool area in May 1909 and then intended to electrify its Manchester suburban network. However the contractor for the Liverpool system, Dick, Kerr & Co of Preston, had its eye on a contract in Brazil and wished to experiment with a high-voltage dc overhead line system, therefore in January 1912 it offered to electrify the Bury to Holcombe Brook branch line on a 3,500V dc overhead conductor system at its own expense — an offer that the LYR Board could not refuse! The line was ideal for the purpose, being single track and some 3¾ miles in length, with gradients as steep as 1 in 40 and the terminus was no less than 525ft above sea level.

Four vehicles were constructed by the LYR at its Newton Heath works in conjunction with Dick, Kerr & Co, comprising two motor coaches numbered 3500/01 and two trailers, Nos 3600/01, all being third class only. A public service commenced on 29 July 1913 and the formation normally consisted of a motor coach and either one or two trailers according to traffic demand. The vehicles were of all-metal construction with alu-

much of the equipment having been ordered and supplied. For these services the Birmingham Carriage & Finance Co Ltd of Saltley built 21 62-ton motorised luggage vans and six trailer coaches which, together with 14 trailer and 60 control trailer coaches from Lancing, were marshalled into 20 five-car units. Each motor luggage van had four 250hp GEC motors and was flanked by trailer and control trailer vehicles. As the neighbouring London & South Western Railway favoured the 660V dc third rail system and had many more route miles so equipped at the time of the 1923 Grouping, it was hardly surprising that the abandonment of the former LBSCR network was announced in 1926 and the last ac trains

LONDON ROAD
22
12
LONDON ROA
20

DAIMLER
JAGUAR
ALTRINCHAM
M 28571 M
25

minium panelling and were 60ft in length, all having a driving compartment and through gangway at each end to give the utmost flexibility of formation. The motor coaches seated 75 and the trailers 85, the difference being created by the provision of a luggage compartment accessed by roller shutters — a feature that has only recently reappeared on BR!

The motor coaches had a pantograph at either end and all axles were motored, those of vehicle No 3500 being rated at 150hp on an 8ft wheelbase bogie whilst

those of No 3501 were of 250hp on a 10ft wheelbase, all at 1,750V and permanently connected in pairs in parallel. In many ways these trains and their Liverpool counterparts were to set the standard for much later designs, not least in breaking away from the concept of compartment-type stock for suburban services. I feel justified, therefore, in illustrating them in some detail although despite this early lead the latter configuration was still used for locomotive-hauled coaches and multiple-unit trains well into BR days.

Meanwhile it had been decided to electrify the Manchester to Bury via Prestwich line, as the first stage in a comprehensive scheme for the area, but it was considered that the erection of overhead line equipment at the Manchester end would be too complicated and a 1,200V dc third rail system was chosen instead (see *BR Fleet Survey 10: Third Rail Electric Multiple-Units*). Therefore when Dick, Kerr & Co had satisfactorily completed its experiments it was decided in 1917 to convert the Holcombe Brook branch to 'match' the Manchester line. However a serious failure in the electrical sub-station brought a premature end to the 3,500V system, and for the last months of its existence services were maintained with the overhead line energised at 1,200V from the Bury to Manchester supply, with the branch train consisting of a 1,200V 'Manchester' motor coach coupled to a 3,500V 'Holcombe Brook' motor coach. The latter merely collected the current

with its pantographs and passed it via jumper cables to the traction motors of the third rail vehicle — a simple short-term solution which avoided the need to renew the sub-station equipment and kept an electric service running until the dc third rail service was introduced on 29 March 1918. The four dc overhead vehicles were then put into store, initially at Bury and then at Horwich, only to reappear in 1928 when the LMSR used them to form the basis of a short-lived experimental diesel-electric train (see *BR Fleet Survey 9*).

Thus it can be seen that the MR pioneered the ac overhead system, whilst the LBSCR and the LYR introduced the corresponding dc system (albeit in the latter case at the expense of Dick, Kerr & Co which, in the event, did not undertake any work in Brazil until 1926). Both systems were to be developed at a later stage — but the foundations had been laid.

There remains one final line to be considered, the Manchester South Junction & Altrincham (MSJA) — jointly owned by the LMSR and LNER since the 1923 Grouping. This was a very busy suburban railway, some nine miles in length and with much of it four track it was an obvious candidate for electrification. One might have expected a dc third rail system to be adopted bearing in mind the existing London and Liverpool lines; however when the scheme was finally approved in 1928 it perhaps anticipated the Weir Report of 1930 and utilised a 1,500V dc overhead line system. At the time only

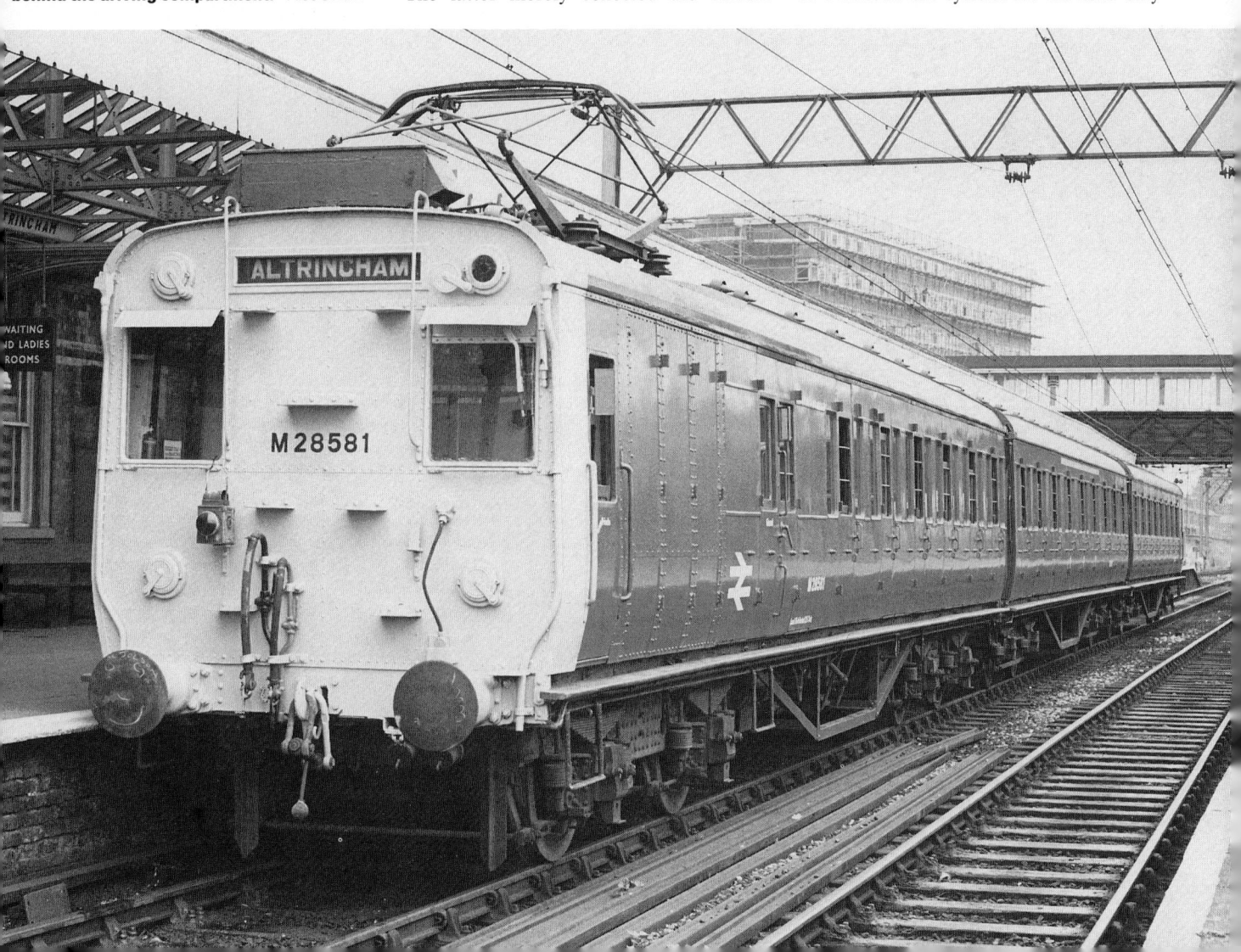

he Newport to Shildon freight line used such a system in Britain although there were others in countries abroad.

The LMSR influence was strong, and the 22 three-car units built by the Metropolitan Carriage & Wagon Co in 1930 were based on the 1927 Euston to Watford compartment stock, and carried a pantograph on the roof above the driving compartment of

the motor coach of which there were in fact 24, allowing for maintenance. Perhaps surprisingly, in view of the short journey times, the intermediate trailer coach included first class accommodation, no doubt for the benefit of the Manchester businessmen who lived in areas such as Sale and who had some influence with the LMSR directors! Public services commenced in May 1931 and, apart from a short-lived experiment in 1939 which added a fourth trailer coach to some units for peak hour services, the trains continued to serve the MSJA travellers until May 1971 with a number even wearing the corporate BR blue livery and logo. By this time the service had been cut back to Oxford Road station, to allow the MSJA platforms at Piccadilly (alias London Road) to be rebuilt extensively in preparation for the link-up with the 25kV system. The units were sold for scrap to a variety of dealers but, happily, three of the trailer coaches (Nos 29663, 29666 and 29670) have survived in the care of the Midland Railway Trust at Butterley and are awaiting restoration. One is the property of Derbyshire City Council and is on lease to the Trust, whilst the other two are privately owned.

Although these trains are not strictly within the subject matter of this book, they did serve well into the BR era and indeed those of the MSJA could be seen alongside their eventual 25kV successors at Oxford

Road. I therefore feel justified in including some details — if for no other reason than my regular use of the latter during a period of employment at Manchester.

MSJA stock

DTS	29231-29252	31t		108S
TC	29390-29396	30t	24F	72S*
	29650-29671	30t	24F	72S
MBS	28571-28594	57t		72S**

* These were the additional vehicles provided in 1939 for the abortive strengthening. With the exception of No 29396, which remained on the MSJA until 1966, the others were converted to locomotive-hauled stock in 1954

** MBS has four 328hp GEC motors

Lancaster to Morecambe stock
Midland Railway

DMS	28610-28612	25t	72S*
DT	29290-29293	18t	56S

* DMS had either two Siemens 180hp or two Westinghouse 150hp motors

LNWR Earls Court conversions

DTS	29021-29024	28t	56S
TS	29721-29742	26t	62S
MBS	28219-28222	57t	28S/28S*

* Nos 28219-28221 had four 215hp EE motors, whilst No 28222 had four MV215 also of 215hp. With the electrical equipment being underslung, the seating capacity of this vehicle could be increased to 38

Nationalisation — The First Years

On 1 January 1948 British Railways inherited a very mixed selection of electrified routes, mostly of a suburban nature using, as we have seen, a variety of methods of current collection etc. A policy for the future was obviously necessary and a 1951 report recommended the 1,500V dc overhead line system favoured by the former LNER and indeed introduced in 1931 on the MSJA line, so the first electrification schemes to be completed were those long planned by that company, and covered the Liverpool Street to Shenfield and Manchester to Sheffield/Wath routes.

Below:
A newly repainted Class 506 unit, with DTS vehicle No M59607M leading, head the 17.29 Hadfield-Manchester at milepost 12 near Dinting on 14 June 1974. *Brian Morrison*

1 MCCW/BRCW Birmingham, ER London Suburban Services, Class 306

Introduced: 1949
Purpose: Liverpool Street to Shenfield services
No of cars per unit: Three
Original unit numbers: 001-092
Present unit numbers: All withdrawn from normal service
Equipment manufacturer: Metrovick
Traction motor type: Crompton Parkinson (four per unit)
Available horsepower: 828hp (620kW)
Maximum speed: 70mph (113km/hr)
Weight of unit: 85.1 tonnes
Length of unit: 52.06m (170ft 9½in)

The 1935 New Works programme, involving the expenditure of some £45 million, authorised the then London Passenger Transport Board to extend its Central Line eastwards from Liverpool Street to Leyton and there link up with the LNER's Ongar and Hainault loop services which it would then electrify and operate. The LNER in turn would then electrify the Liverpool Street to Shenfield section of the Norwich main line, but using the recommended 1,500V dc system. Work had commenced but the outbreak of war in 1939 brought this to a halt and it was not resumed until early 1946. By March 1949 some trial running was possible, although by this time the line formed part of the Eastern Region.

The 92 three-car units (DMBS-TS-DTS) required to work the intensive service were built by Metropolitan-Cammell Carriage & Wagon Co (MCCW), (DMBS and TS vehicles) and the Birmingham Railway Carriage & Wagon Co (BRCW) (DTS vehicles). Construction was under the overall direction of A. H. Peppercorn, Chief Mechanical Engineer of the Eastern and North Eastern Regions, and these were the last multiple-unit trains to be developed in this manner prior to the setting up of a central BR authority for new rolling stock construction.

To accommodate the trains a new depot was constructed to the east of Ilford station, partly on the site of the triangular junction which connected to Newbury Park and the Hainault loop, and it is interesting to relate this approach to that of the 'make do and mend' attitude which prevailed in later years as modern traction was introduced elsewhere on BR!

The trains were modern in design in that passenger-operated powered sliding doors

Below:
A new Shenfield line unit poses at Ilford depot bearing an optimistic destination, as the projected service from Stratford to Fenchurch Street never came to fruition. Note the set/duty number on the front end in the form of a removable disc or 'target'.
Colin Marsden collection

Below right:
A Shenfield service running on the down fast line passes under the Ilford flyover, which carries the slow lines, on 21 April 1951.
R. E. Vincent

were provided, with capacity for 168 seated passengers in an open saloon environment far removed from that of the steam-hauled compartment stock that generations of Essex commuters had had to endure, and this electrification scheme — like all those that have followed to the present day — produced a healthy increase in traffic.

The build of 92 trains included a number for a projected Fenchurch Street to Stratford service which never materialised and this surplus enabled the service to be extended to Chelmsford in June 1956. It is of interest to record that one of the bay platforms provided, but never used, at Stratford now accommodates the trains of the Docklands Light Railway, albeit operating on a 750V dc under-contact third rail system!

Thus the Shenfield units, later to be known as Class 306, continued about their daily business until 1959 when they were progressively withdrawn from service for conversion to 6.25/25kV ac following the decision that this was to be the future standard for BR electrification. The lower voltage had been deemed necessary when, in heavily built-up areas, the costs of raising bridges or structures to give suitable clearance for 25kV operation could not be justified.

The conversion work was undertaken at Stratford works, using electrical equipment supplied by Metrovick, and required some quite drastic surgery to fit the trains for their new role. The original pantograph previously carried above the driving compartment of the DMBS vehicle was removed and replaced by a single-arm type mounted on the specially-lowered roof of the TS vehicle. The roof of the now-DMS vehicle then had to be built-up to match the main profile, whilst the guard and luggage compartments were removed to extend the passenger saloon, alternative accommodation being provided in the now-TBS vehicle. The necessary transformer, rectifier and other equipment required for ac operation were fitted but not connected to enable each converted unit to return to its dc role temporarily whilst another took its place.

The conversion to 6.25/25kV ac operation took place early in November 1960, and in the ensuing weeks the trains were again progressively withdrawn from service to enable the ac equipment to be connected. In this form they continued to give good service although, in 1976, replacement trains were authorised in the shape of Class 315 units. However, developments and tests had indicated that 25kV

was, after all, suitable for use in areas with limited structural clearances and that the automatic dual voltage changeover equipment carried on units could be dispensed with.

Therefore the Class 315 specification was amended to provide for 25kV only and, with the overhead line finally energised at this voltage throughout from Liverpool Street to Shenfield and Southend in October 1980, the last Class 306 units were withdrawn in 1981. Many were stored at Stanway sidings, just to the south of Colchester, prior to being sent to various scrap dealers, whilst one unit, No 306017, has been retained at Ilford depot for special workings and has been restored to the original BR multiple-unit green livery, albeit with yellow warning panels.

Details of Class 306: Built 1949, rebuilt 1960/61

DMS	18.41×2.90m	51.7t	62S
TBS	16.78×2.90m	26.4t	46S
DTS	16.87×2.90m	27.9t	60S

Sets numbered 001-092

DMS	numbered 65201-65292*
TBS	numbered 65401-65492
DTS	numbered 65601-65692

* DMS has four CP 270hp motors

Left:

For the conversion to 6.25/25kV operation, extensive rebuilding was necessary, as shown by former DMBS vehicle No 65238 of set No 38 at Stratford works on 30 April 1960, resting on temporary bogies. The roof profile has been restored following the removal of the pantograph, and the former guard's compartment has been removed and replaced by passenger accommodation. An aperture has been cut for the two-digit headcode panel which has replaced the four marker lights.
Alec Swain

Left:

Similar surgery was necessary for the TS vehicles, and here No 65438 at Stratford works on 30 April 1960 shows the extent of the rebuild. A 'well' has been provided for the pantograph and a new guard's compartment has been fashioned out of former passenger accommodation. Extra ventilation grilles have been provided on the bodyside.
Alec Swain

Below:

The pride of Ilford depot, the restored Class 306 unit No 017 in green livery, stands at Seven Kings on Network Day, 22 November 1986, working the first shuttle service to Shenfield. *John B. Gosling*

2 MCCW/BRCW Birmingham, LMR Manchester Suburban Services, Class 506

Introduced: 1954
Purpose: Manchester to Glossop/Hadfield services
No of cars per unit: Three
Original unit numbers: 001-008
Present unit numbers: All withdrawn
Equipment manufacturer: GEC
Traction motor type: GEC (four per unit)
Available horsepower: 740hp (555kW)
Maximum speed: 70mph (113km/hr)
Weight of unit: 107 tonnes
Length of unit: 52.06m (170ft 9½in)

The electrification of the LNER route between Manchester (London Road) and Sheffield, together with the Glossop branch, had been approved in 1936 and work was well advanced on the 1,500V dc system before the outbreak of war in 1939 effectively stopped it. Work was resumed in the late 1940s and on Nationalisation in 1948 the route, Manchester to Sheffield/Wath (MSW) became part of the Eastern Region. However, from April 1950, the section of line west of Dunford Bridge passed to the London Midland Region and the eight three-car units, to the same LNER design as the Shenfield units, entered service in June 1954 under control of that Region.

The units were formed DMBS-TS-DTS, and again the DMBS and TS vehicles were built by MCCW with the DTS vehicles being the work of BRCW. They were based at a purpose-built depot at Reddish, together with the electric locomotives which operated the other passenger and freight services. Although trials were conducted with a view to their working through to Sheffield, problems with the overheating of the traction motors on the long climb to Woodhead together with clearance problems east of Penistone (the vehicles were 9ft 3in wide) precluded this and they spent all their life working the Hadfield and Glossop services.

The controversial decision to close the Woodhead route, following the withdrawal of the remaining Manchester to Sheffield passenger services in January 1970, was eventually implemented in July 1981, which meant that the Class 506 units, as they had now become, were the last 1,500V dc multiple-unit trains in BR service (the Altrincham service having ceased in April 1971). With the closure of Reddish depot in May 1983 this meant that the units had to be hauled 'dead' to Longsight depot for maintenance, which had not previously dealt with dc traction. It was inevitable therefore, in view of their age, that conversion to ac could not be justified and the release of a number of

Below:
The first Hadfield train enters Manchester London Road on 12 May 1954 during trials prior to the start of the public service in June of that year. Note the interested onlookers, not least of whom were the crew of the former GCR 'C13' 4-4-2T standing alongside.
B. K. B. Green

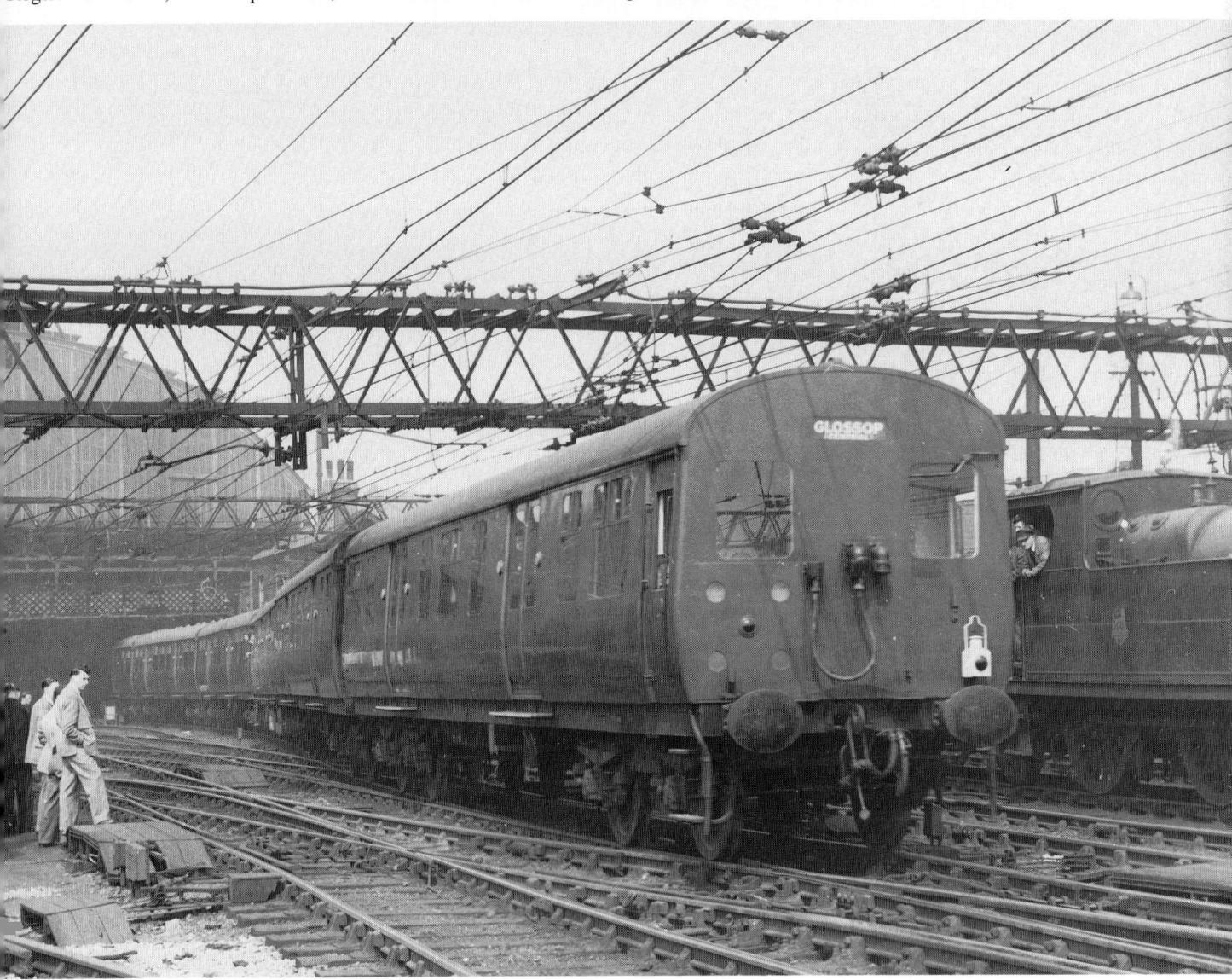

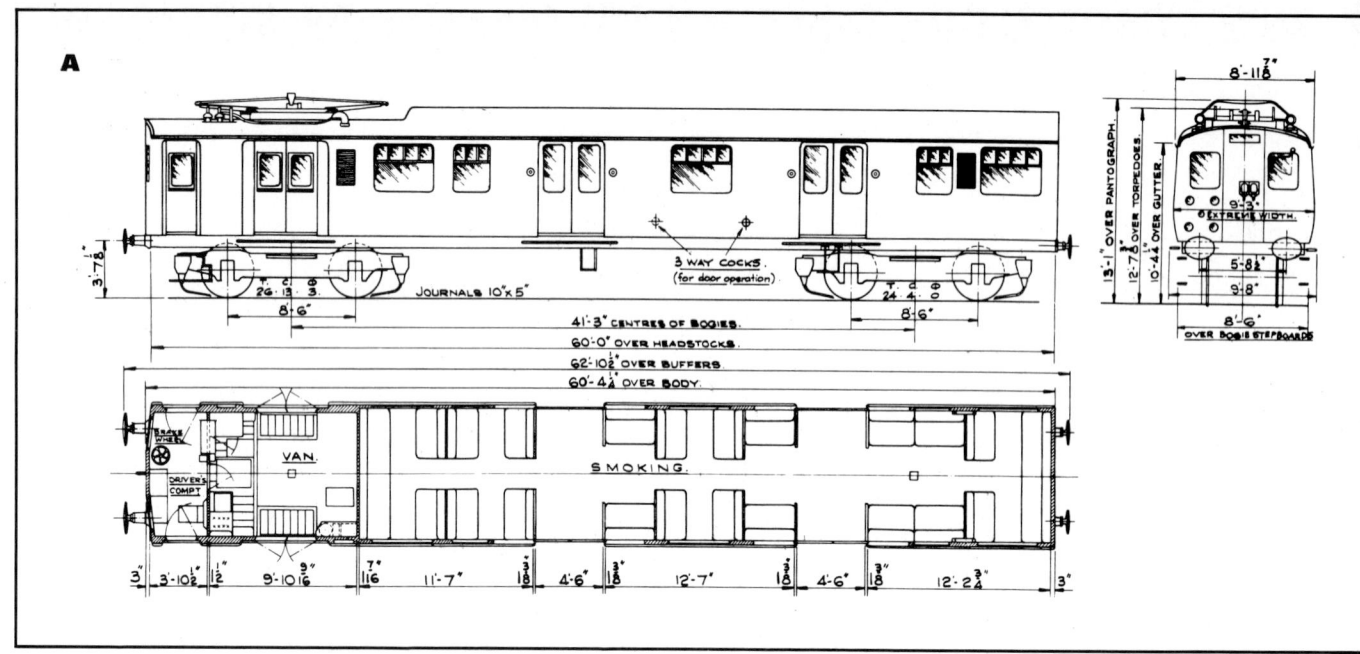

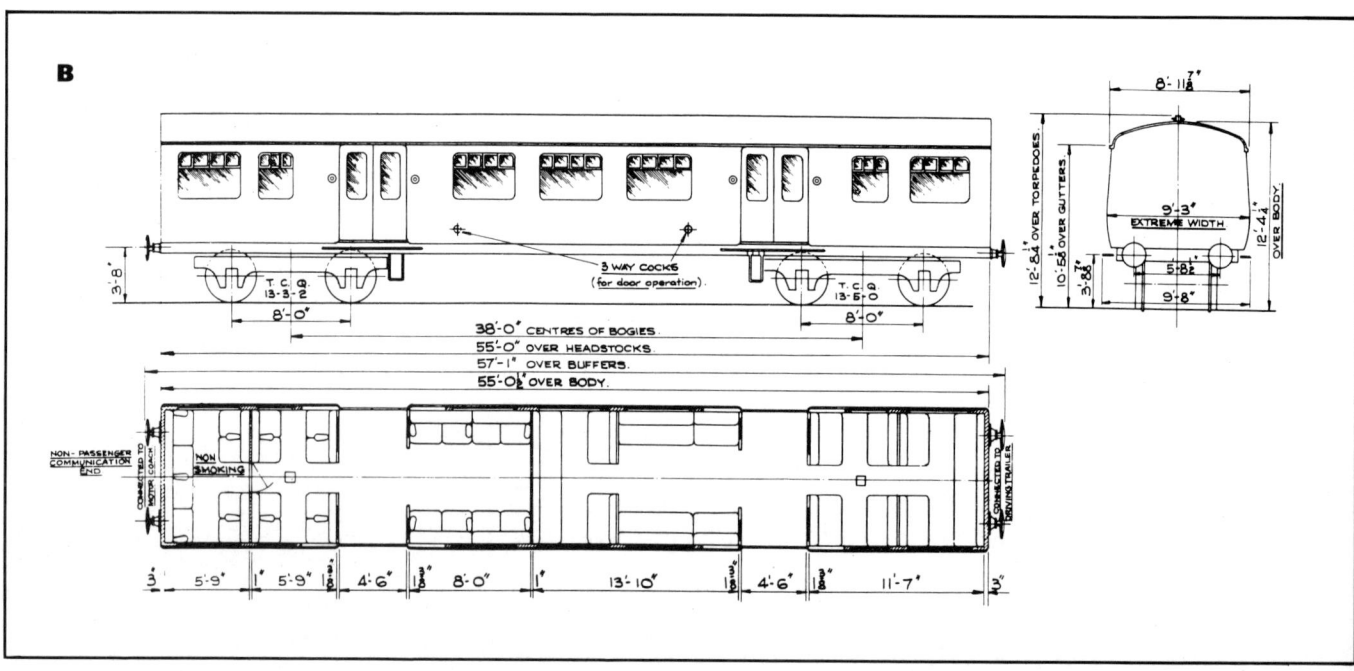

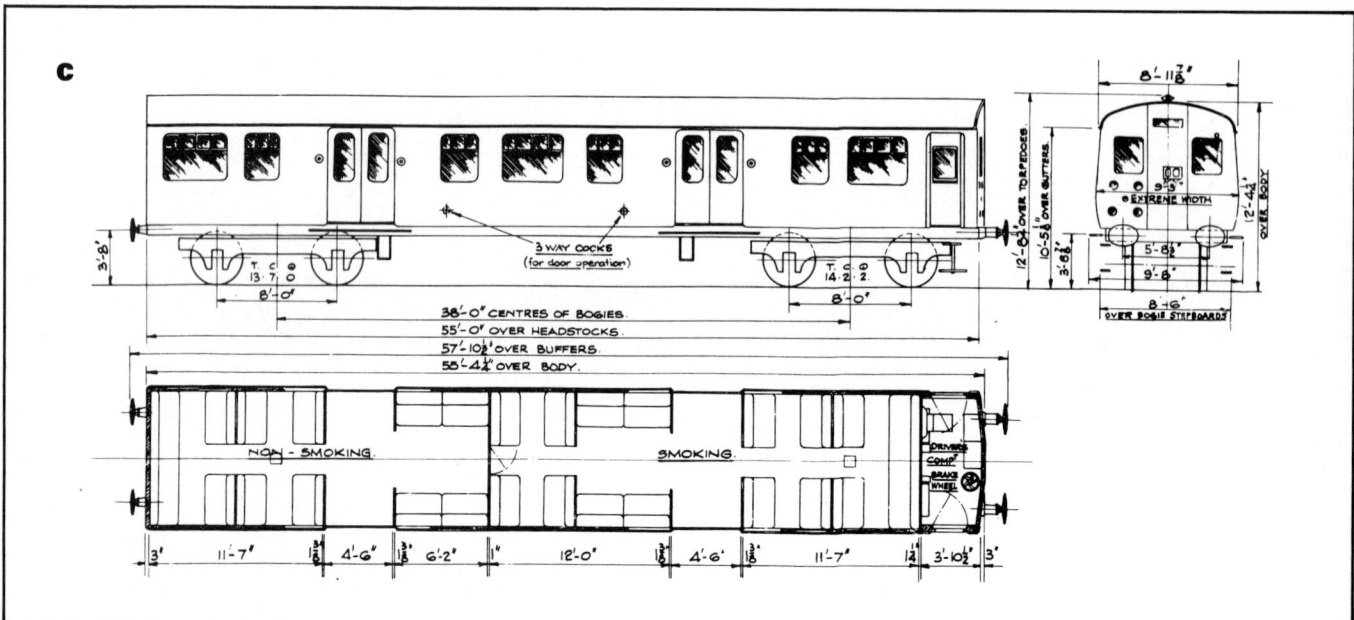

ScR Class 303 units enabled the remaining stub of the MSW system to be converted to 25kV ac and the last Class 506 units operated on 7 December 1984. One unit, comprising vehicles Nos 59404, 59504 and 59604, has been acquired by the West Yorkshire Transport Museum for possible operation on a reopened Spen Valley Railway through Cleckheaton and Heckmondwike, whilst the remainder made their last journey to a Leicester scrapyard. After initial storage at the former Bradford Hammerton Street DMU depot, the preserved unit was moved to the Midland Railway Centre at Butterley in May 1989.

Details of Class 506: Built 1954

DMBS	18.41×2.90m	51.6t	52S
TS	16.78×2.90m	26.5t	56S
DTS	16.87×2.90m	27.9t	60S
DMBS	numbered 59401-59408*		
TS	numbered 59501-59508		
DTS	numbered 59601-59608		

* DMBS has four GEC 185hp motors

Left:
The three vehicles of a Class 506 unit: (A) DMBS (B) TS (C) DTS, which were highly similar to those of Class 306 prior to the latter's rebuilding. Note that the bogies of the DMBS vehicle are shown equipped with sanding apparatus and that the TS has, in fact, two separate saloon areas with a dividing partition. Passengers certainly had a choice of seating! *BR*

Top right:
In 1957 tests were conducted with a view to the service being extended to Sheffield, and a unit is shown here entering Penistone station on 20 September of that year. Concern over possible overheating of the traction motors on the long climb to Woodhead Tunnel and slight clearance problems east of Penistone led to the proposal being abandoned and the trains did not work regularly beyond Hadfield. *B. K. B. Green*

Centre right:
In green livery with small yellow warning panel, DTS No M59603M heads an afternoon departure for Hadfield at Manchester Piccadilly on 12 August 1968, with a two-car DMU train at the opposite platform.
Alec Swain

Below right:
The rain-soaked platforms of Guide Bridge play host to a westbound Class 506 unit on 8 April 1983, with DMBS vehicle No M59404M nearest the camera. The unit is in the blue/grey livery with a combined logo for the Greater Manchester PTE.
Graham Scott-Lowe

Top:
A Class 506 unit in blue livery, with DTS vehicle No M59607M leading, awaits departure from Manchester Piccadilly on 23 August 1980. Note that the marker lights remained in use. *Peter Harris*

Above:
Following the closure of Reddish depot on 16 May 1983, the Class 506 units were maintained at Longsight. On 29 May a three-car unit headed by DMBS No M59404M receives attention alongside a Class 86 25kV electric locomotive. There was no 1,500V dc catenary so the units had to be diesel-hauled to and from Piccadilly with adequate precautions to ensure that the pantographs were not raised! *Richard Fox*

Left:
The Class 506 unit preserved by the West Yorkshire Transport Museum, with vehicle No M59404M leading, stored within the former Bradford Hammerton Street DMU depot. It was moved to the Midland Railway Centre, Butterley in May 1989.
West Yorkshire Transport Museum

The First Generation BR Overhead Line EMU Designs

The development of the BR Standard EMU is described in great detail in Part 10 of this series, and is equally applicable to the overhead line classes, so once again I do not intend to cover the same ground other than to record the three basic types of unit that were decided upon:

1 A high density suburban layout with both open saloons and conventional compartments, no gangways between vehicles and no toilets

2 An outer suburban layout basically similar with some first class compartments with side corridor access and toilet facilities, but again no gangways between vehicles

3 An express passenger layout, similar to locomotive-hauled stock, with a mixture of open saloons and first class compartments together with refreshment facilities as required. Gangwayed throughout, including the driving end vehicles, to enable passengers to have access to the whole train

These basic designs have stood the test of time, and only as the classes are refurbished has it been deemed necessary to provide inter-vehicle gangway connections and to convert the compartment areas to open saloon layout. There are obvious advantages in this; it enables passengers to find seats in a less-crowded part of the train, it gives the opportunity for on-train revenue protection duties and finally, with the abolition of compartments, it is a deterrent to those intent on vandalism and crime. The remaining compart ..t stock now has a red line painted above the windows to indicate to persons not wishing to risk travelling in such accommodation that they should find seats elsewhere in the train. Some thought was given to the restoration of 'ladies only' compartments but the difficulty of enforcing such a restriction, given the present-day manning levels at stations, caused this to be abandoned.

In retrospect it is a pity that saloon-type seating and power-operated doors were not specified; nevertheless the management of the day no doubt had the remit to provide a similar number of seats to that of the locomotive-hauled stock being replaced and, bearing in mind the limitations of platform lengths and the financial and chronological constraints of the Modernisation Plan, it is perhaps no wonder that existing designs were adapted, although there were exceptions as we shall see!

However, the choice and subsequent development of 25kV ac electrification did raise the problem of the minimum clearance that would be necessary to ensure safety when the overhead line had to pass under bridges, through tunnels etc, and it was decreed that the clearance must be 23in. Since the civil engineering work necessary to provide this clearance in built-up areas such as city centres and suburbs would have been prohibitively expensive it was decided that if only 6.25kV were to be used the clearance could be reduced to 11in and thus there came into being the unique 6.25/25kV ac dual voltage system. This required the provision of special equipment on all the early multiple-unit trains destined for the London and Glasgow suburban services which would detect the voltage in the overhead line at the 6.25/25kV boundary points in conjunction with the automatic power control (APC) system.

The APC system is necessary because the overhead line is energised by a number of feeder stations on the route, each supplying its designated length, with a neutral section in the overhead line separating them. A neutral section is electrically 'dead' and to automatically discontinue the power supply to the main transformer, and hence the traction motors, before the pantograph reaches the neutral section APC magnets are positioned on the sleeper ends well in advance. The presence of these is detected by APC receivers mounted on one of the bogies and the control circuitry opens the main circuit breaker of the train to effect the disconnection. Beyond the neutral section further APC magnets on the sleeper ends are detected by the train's receivers, which now close the main circuit breaker and thus automatically reconnect the transformer to the now-live overhead line, no action at all being required on the part of the driver. The procedure at a

Below:
The first generation BR Standard EMU incorporating the high density suburban layout specified. 'AM5' unit No 409 is seen when new in the works yard at York on 11 May 1960, with DTS No E75522 leading. Each DTS vehicle provided 94 seats, whilst the MBS could muster 84, giving a total seating capacity of 272 for a three-car unit.
BR

6.25/25kV boundary point was similar except that before the main circuit breaker was closed to reconnect the supply a special detection circuit measured the voltage in the overhead line and if, say, 6.25kV was found to be present, a voltage changeover switch made the appropriate connection on the input to the main transformer to suit that voltage. This system was first used in Glasgow and applied to the 'Blue Trains' but with disastrous consequences as we shall see in Section 5. Although the problems were overcome it was obviously desirable to reduce, and eventually eliminate, the number of voltage changeover points, and following further tests, new clearances and insulation standards were approved in 1962 which enabled the WCML from Euston to Manchester and Liverpool to be electrified at 25kV throughout – no doubt to the intense relief of those concerned! This had an effect on the design of new units, particularly Class 315 as we shall see in Section 14, and it was not until 21 May 1989 that the final 6.25kV sections were eliminated – those from Fenchurch Street to East Ham and from Leigh to Shoeburyness.

One other factor to influence the life of these first generation BR designs was the presence of blue asbestos, which had been freely used for many years as insulation within the bodysides and vehicle ends. However, medical evidence later showed that the fibres, if inhaled, could be detrimental to health and a programme of asbestos removal, or withdrawal of the affected vehicles, was quickly drawn up and agreed with the trade unions, who were naturally concerned over the possible risk to their members. As long as the insulation remained undisturbed there were no immediate problems, although its presence did lead to the sealing of the access to the destination indicators on Class 302 and 307 units which therefore remained unchanged! The removal of the offending substance had to be undertaken by specialists wearing protective clothing, thus decisions had to be taken as to whether or not such work was financially justified taking into account the life

expectancy of the class in question. Even the disposal of withdrawn vehicles proved a problem and specialist scrap dealers had to set up special incinerators into which the vehicles were placed. The intense heat released the asbestos fibres which were then washed free by high pressure hoses and left to settle in sediment tanks before final collection. Much of this was undertaken at the time of refurbishment of the various classes, which required stripping down to the bare bodyshell anyway, and the internal corrosion which was then revealed often led to the withdrawal of a particular vehicle and its substitution by another in better condition. This is a practice that is still prevalent today when maintenance depots hold a 'pool' of spare vehicles, possibly the result of collision or derailment damage to a unit, leaving some virtually undamaged or at least repairable within financial limits. Thus the enthusiast of today who seeks to record the formations of multiple-unit trains, diesel or electric, is kept quite busy!

Below:
The express specification was very similar to the locomotive-hauled stock of the time, with a mixture of open saloons and first class compartments, but with end gangways to permit passenger access throughout the length of the train. Here 'AM9' buffet unit No 616 is seen at Clacton on 25 May 1963, with DTC vehicle No GE75642 leading (18 first, 32 standard seats), followed by MBS (48 standard seats), Trailer Buffet (32 seats) and DTC (18 first, 32 standard seats), totalling 36 first and 144 standard.
Brian Haresnape

Bottom:
The outer suburban specification called for toilet facilities and some first class accommodation, here provided by 'AM8' unit No 144 with the 11.30 Liverpool Street-Clacton near Colchester on 22 August 1964. The DTS vehicle with toilet is leading (80 seats), next the MBS (96 seats), followed by the TC (19 first, 60 standard seats with toilets) and the DTS (108 seats). Thus the four-car unit provided 19 first and 344 standard seats and, provided the passenger knew which vehicle to board (as there were no gangways within the unit when built), the necessary facilities! *J. C. Beckett*

3 BR Ashford/Eastleigh, ER London Outer Suburban Services, Class 307

Introduced: 1956
Purpose: Liverpool Street to Southend services
No of cars per unit: Four
Original unit numbers: 101-132
Present unit numbers: 307101-307132
Equipment manufacturer: GEC
Traction motor type: GEC WT344 (four per unit)
Available horsepower: 696hp (520kW)
Maximum speed: 75mph (120km/hr)
Weight of unit: 154.7 tonnes
Length of unit: 80.975m (265ft 8in)

When the new trains for the Liverpool Street to Southend electrified service were unveiled in 1956, ready for the commencement of electric services in December of that year, there must have been a number of raised eyebrows in certain quarters as there had been a reversion to slam-door stock and the operating authorities of the time must have regretted the fact that they could not work in multiple with the Shenfield (Class 306) units with which the track and maintenance facilities were shared. It was no doubt a matter of expediency that they were built to the SR

standard 'EPB' style with perhaps the only concession being a choice of seating layout. As built they were formed DTS-MBS-TC-DTS, with the pantograph being carried on the MBS vehicle above the guard's compartment. Their conversion to 6.25/25kV ac operation during 1960/61 required quite extensive rebuilding, not unlike that of the Class 306 units, with the guard's compartment and new pantograph being installed at the inner end of one of the former DTS vehicles, together with a new transformer and rectifier on the underframe. The vehicle thus became classified DTBS. The former MBS vehicle simply became MS and retained its original dc control and traction equipment. In this form the units returned to dc work for a period.

However, in November 1960 they were all taken out of service and their place was taken by trains destined for the Fenchurch Street electrification (Class 302) whilst the necessary connections were made to bring the ac equipment into use. Once this was

done they returned to their Southend duties and progressively released the Class 302 units.

The most significant alterations to these units occurred from 1981 onwards however, when a programme of refurbishment started, with the aim of bringing them up to modern standards of passenger comfort. They were gangwayed within the unit, which required a revised internal layout, fitted with fluorescent lighting and new seating and equiped with public address. Previously 19 first class seats had been provided in the TC vehicle and now this accommodation was to be found, increased to 24 seats, in the now-DTC with only a single toilet compartment towards the centre of the vehicle. The MS, in common with the remaining vehicles, became a saloon and thus the revised formation became BDTBS-MS-TS-DTC and no doubt the better environment, together with the provision of B4/B5 bogies to give a better ride, compensated for the loss of 54 standard class seats!

Below:
A brand-new unit in plain green livery, then numbered 05s with DTS vehicle No E75105 leading, poses for the official photographer in Southend Victoria carriage sidings on 16 April 1956. The bow-type pantograph is positioned on the motor coach, with the guard's compartment immediately below. Note the speedometer drive taken from the rear axle of the leading bogie. *GEC*

Details of Class 307: Built Ashford/Eastleigh 1954-56, rebuilt 1961

BDTBS	19.50×2.82m	43.0t		66S	B5	bogies
MS	19.36×2.82m	47.5t		98S	ED7	bogies
TS	19.36×2.82m	31.0t		86S	B4	bogies
DTC	19.50×2.82m	33.0t	24F	52S	B4	bogies

Sets numbered 307101-307132 all refurbished

BDTBS numbered 75001-75032
MS numbered 61001-61032*
TS numbered 70001-70032
DTC numbered 75101-75132

*MS has four GEC WT344 130kW motors

A

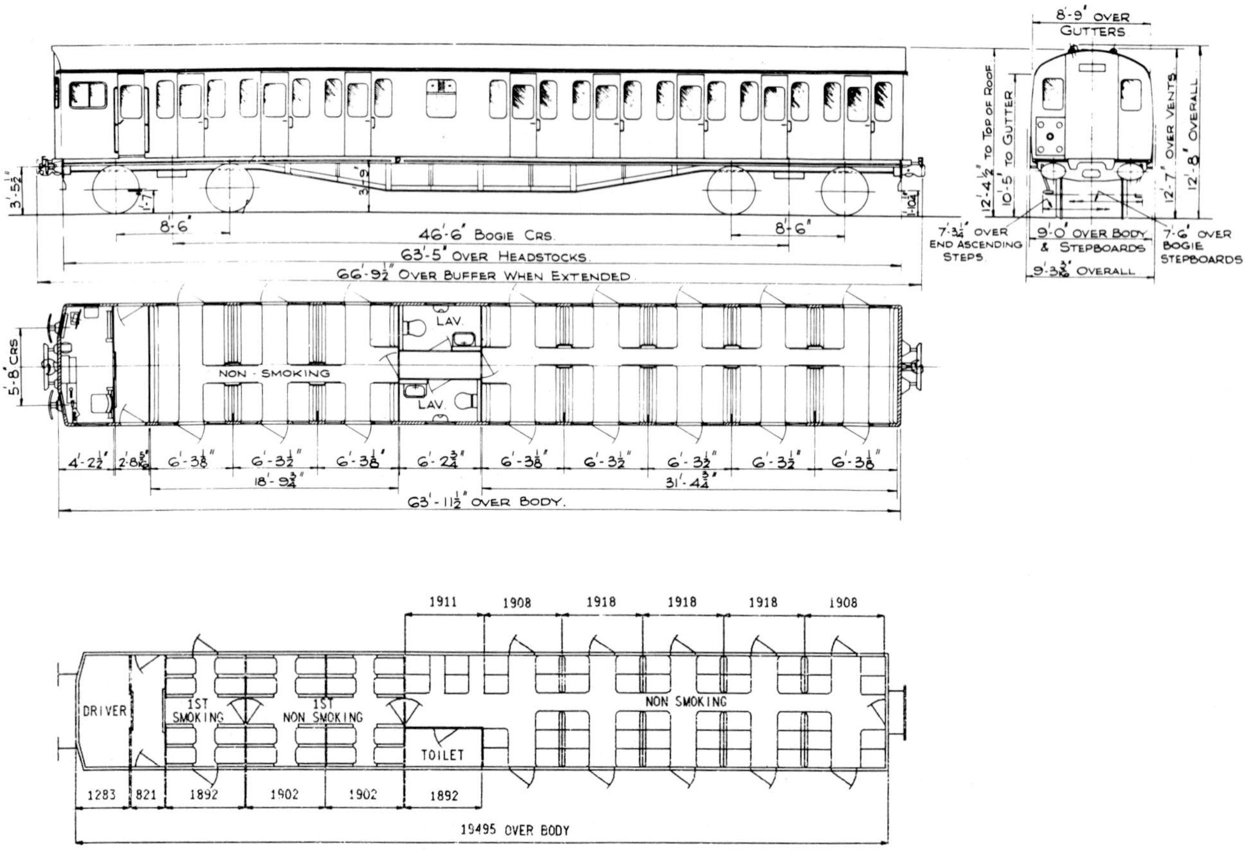

8'-9" OVER GUTTERS

46'-6" BOGIE CRS.
63'-5" OVER HEADSTOCKS
66'-9½" OVER BUFFER WHEN EXTENDED

8'-6" 8'-6"

NON-SMOKING LAV. LAV.

5'-8" CRS

4'-2½" 2'-8⅝" 6'-3⅜" 6'-3½" 6'-3⅜" 6'-2¾" 6'-3⅜" 6'-3½" 6'-3½" 6'-3⅜"
18'-9¾" 31'-4⅝"
63'-11½" OVER BODY.

12'-4½" TO TOP OF ROOF
10'-5" TO GUTTER
12'-7" OVER VENTS
12'-8" OVERALL

7'-3¼" OVER END ASCENDING STEPS 9'-0" OVER BODY & STEPBOARDS 7'-6" OVER BOGIE STEPBOARDS
9'-3¾" OVERALL

| 1911 | 1908 | 1918 | 1918 | 1918 | 1908 |

DRIVER 1ST SMOKING 1ST NON SMOKING TOILET NON SMOKING

1283 821 1892 1902 1902 1892

19495 OVER BODY

B

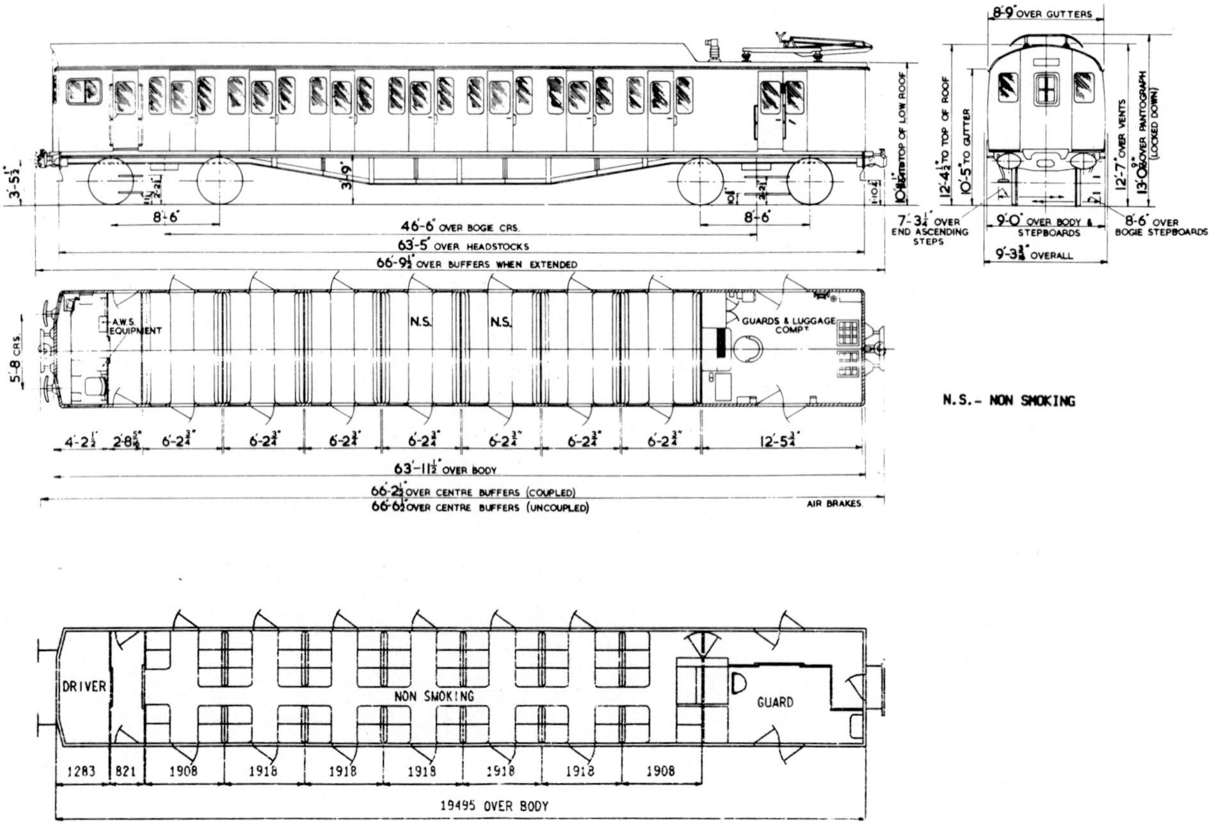

8'-9" OVER GUTTERS

46'-6" OVER BOGIE CRS.
63'-5" OVER HEADSTOCKS
66'-9½" OVER BUFFERS WHEN EXTENDED

8'-6" 8'-6"

A.W.S. EQUIPMENT N.S. N.S. GUARDS & LUGGAGE COMP'T

5'-8" CRS

N.S. – NON SMOKING

4'-2½" 2'-8⅝" 6'-2¾" 6'-2¾" 6'-2¾" 6'-2¾" 6'-2¾" 6'-2¾" 12'-5¾"
63'-11½" OVER BODY
66'-2¾" OVER CENTRE BUFFERS (COUPLED)
66'-6½" OVER CENTRE BUFFERS (UNCOUPLED)

AIR BRAKES

12'-4½" TO TOP OF ROOF
10'-5" TO GUTTER
12'-7" OVER VENTS
13'-0" OVER PANTOGRAPH (LOCKED DOWN)

7'-3¼" OVER END ASCENDING STEPS 9'-0" OVER BODY & STEPBOARDS 8'-6" OVER BOGIE STEPBOARDS
9'-3¾" OVERALL

DRIVER NON SMOKING GUARD

1283 821 1908 1918 1918 1918 1918 1918 1908

19495 OVER BODY

Left:
When the Class 307 units were refurbished there were quite extensive alterations to the seating layout and whilst space does not permit an illustration of each vehicle, these 'before and after' drawings of (A) the DTS vehicle (which became DTC) and (B) the BDTS vehicle will show the effect of the relocation of facilities and the fitting of inter-vehicle gangway connections. *BR*

Above:
This close-up of DTS vehicle No E75105 clearly shows its SR 'EPB' ancestry, with only the destination indicator, marker light display and jumper cable arrangement to identify it as ER owned. *GEC*

Right:
Class 307 unit No 104, now modified for 6. 25/25kV operation and in blue livery with full yellow ends, arrives at Ilford with a Liverpool Street train on 15 September 1980. The marker lights have been replaced by a four-digit route indicator and the jumper cables and brake hoses have been relocated.
John Fozard

Introduced: 1958
Purpose: Fenchurch Street to Shoeburyness services
No of cars per unit: Four
Original unit numbers: 201-312
Present unit numbers: 302200-302299 (with gaps)
Equipment manufacturer: English Electric
Traction motor type: EE 536A (four per unit)
Available horsepower: 770hp (574kW)
Maximum speed: 75mph (120km/hr)
Weight of unit: 155.23 tonnes (162.6 tonnes when refurbished)
Length of unit: 80.975m (265ft 8in)

Once the Liverpool Street to Southend line had been electrified, pressures were exerted similarly to equip the Fenchurch Street to Shoeburyness route including the Tilbury loop, and no less than 112 four-car units were ordered. This line had been built by the London Tilbury & Southend Railway (LTSR), and was taken over by the MR prior to the 1923 Grouping when it became LMSR and therefore passed to the LMR upon nationalisation in 1948. However, in February 1949 it was transferred to the ER and featured in its electrification programme in due course. Known to railwaymen as the 'LTS stock' prior to the

allocation of TOPS classification 302, the units had all been delivered by mid-1960 and the majority were in store pending completion of the electrification works, having seen use on the Colchester to Clacton electrified local services from April 1959 onwards.

As mentioned in Sections 1 and 3 they proved useful as substitutes whilst the Class 306 and 307 units were prepared for ac operation, but this delayed the inauguration of the LTSR service and, although limited peak hour electric working was introduced early in November 1961, no doubt to appease the commuters, it was not until June 1962 that the full benefits were obtained. However, in the winter of 1961 it soon became apparent to the LTSR commuter that all was not well with their new trains and failures became frequent, which must have puzzled the engineers of those days as the units had operated without troubles on the interim Colchester to Clacton/Walton services and as the substitutes mentioned above. So serious were the failures and such was the public outcry that a Ministry of Transport inquiry was carried out by Brig C. A. Langley, Chief Inspecting Officer of Railways, which covered Glasgow's problems as well – but more on these later. The failures

mainly concerned the traction motors, battery chargers and rectifiers, with suspicions centring upon the voltage changeover from 6.25 to 25kV, and the Report, and the contemporary press, make interesting reading. The problems were overcome but involved expensive modifications and the replacement of equipment; however it did lead to a fresh look at the real need for 6.25kV sections of line.

Based at the purpose-built East Ham depot, the units are similar to those of Class 307 and are formed DTS-TC-MBS-BDTS, but have now undergone a two-stage refurbishment programme. What came to be known as the interim refurbishment, begun in 1982 and applied to 79 units, resulted in the DTS and MBS being converted from compart-

Below:
A similar programme of refurbishment has been applied to the Class 302 units, although it has not yet been completed, and the drawing shows the 'before and after' layout of the TC vehicle, now TS, which is equally applicable to those vehicles marshalled in Class 305/2 and 308//1 units. Note that the former first class accommodation, with exclusive toilet, has been removed and relocated elsewhere in the train. *BR*

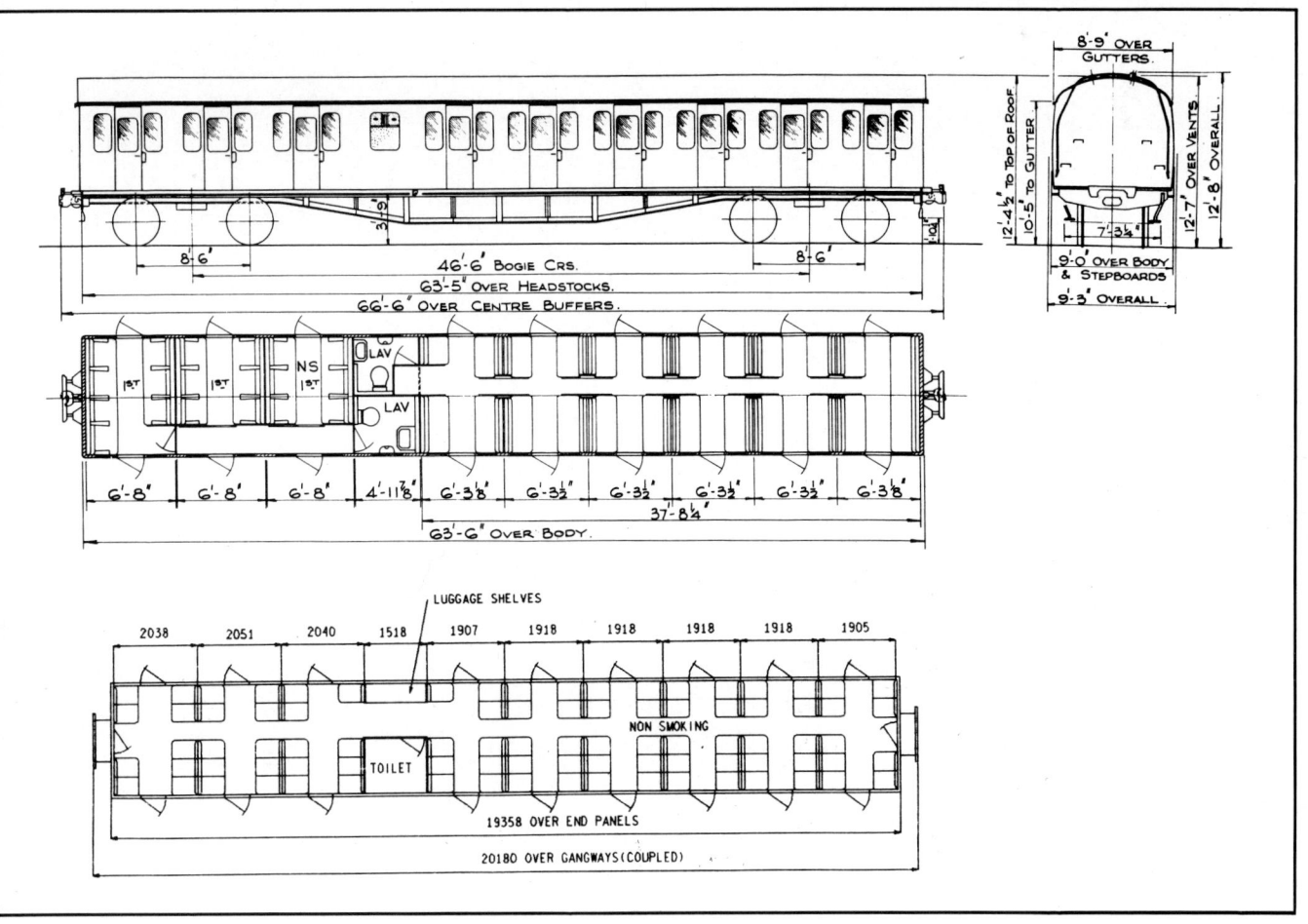

ment to open saloon arrangement with the loss, naturally of 30 standard class seats. Subsequently from 1985 a fuller refurbishment incorporating inter-vehicle gangways has taken place, to the same standards as that applied to Class 307, resulting in the loss of a further 12 standard class seats and a revised formation DTS-TS-MBS-BDTC, and these units are now numbered 302201-302230.

At the moment the opportunity is being taken to withdraw many of the units that have not had the benefit of either refurbishment programme, particularly those vehicles with compartment accommodation and retaining blue asbestos insulation. On behalf of the Parcels Sector, Ilford depot has produced three three-car units, Nos 302990-302992, which are now in GPO red livery and carry the legend 'Royal Mail'. Using former DTS and MBS vehicles which have been gutted internally, they are equipped with roller shutter doors to facilitate the loading and unloading of mailbags. For Departmental use as a 'Sandite' train, three-car unit No 302996 has been assembled and is used to apply this anti-slip/slide medium to the running rails to improve adhesion, particularly during the leaf-fall season.

Details of Class 302P: Built York/Doncaster 1958-60

BDTC	19.50×2.82m	39.5t	24F	52S	B5	bogies
MBS	19.36×2.82m	55.3t		76S	GM	bogies (Gresley)
TS	19.36×2.82m	34.4t		86S	B4	bogies
DTS	19.50×2.82m	33.4t		88S	B4	bogies

Sets	numbered	302201-302230 refurbished
		302200, 231-299 with gaps
		302990-302992 Parcels Sector use
		302996 Departmental use
BDTC	numbered	75085-75210
		75286-75360
MBS	numbered	61060-61228*
TS	numbered	70060-70227
DTS	numbered	75033-75084
		75211-75284

*MBS has four EE536A 143.5kW motors

Note that unit reformations and renumbering following refurbishment or allocation to Department or Sector use has upset the original numerical allocation of vehicles to units.

Below:
In 1959 the line between Colchester and Clacton, together with the branch to Walton, was electrified at 25kV — the first application of what was to be the standard for BR. Units eventually intended for the LTSR section, and which later became Class 302, were utilised such as No 247 depicted here with DTS vehicle No E75295 leading. *P. Ransome Wallis/Ian Allan Library*

Right:
In 1982 a programme which became known as the interim refurbishment commenced, and 79 Class 302 units were so treated, including unit No 207 which has been restored to green livery with the small yellow warning panel, seen here in the bay platform at Upminster with DTS vehicle No 75039 nearest the camera. Note that no marker lights were fitted during this programme, the former route indicator being blanked off to display just two white dots. *Peter Marsh*

Below right:
Late 1984 saw a further refurbishment programme commence, but this time marker lights were fitted and the route indicator removed. Here Class 302 unit No 302263 is far from home, on exhibition to the West Midlands PTE at Birmingham International on 23 November 1984, with Class 310 unit No 310092 alongside. Note that despite the provision of two red tail lights on this stock, an oil tail lamp is still deemed necessary! *John B. Gosling*

Below, far right:
Class 302 unit No 302261 calls at Grays on 27 May 1989 with a Shoeburyness service. The absence of marker lights and the retention of the route indicator, albeit showing two white dots, identifies it as a unit that had the interim refurbishment only, ie prior to 1985. *Alec Swain*

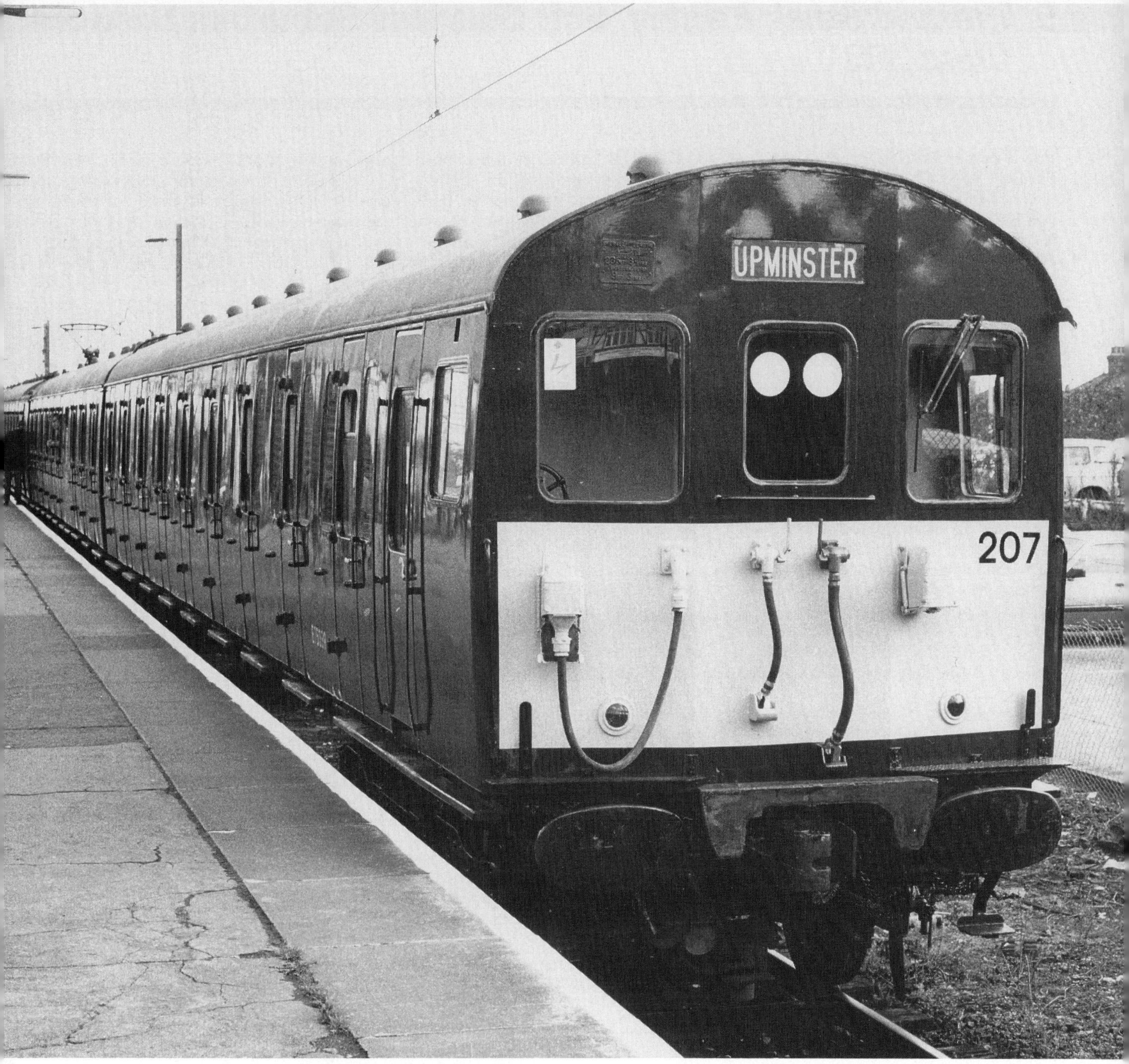
UPMINSTER
207

Special
302
263

302
261

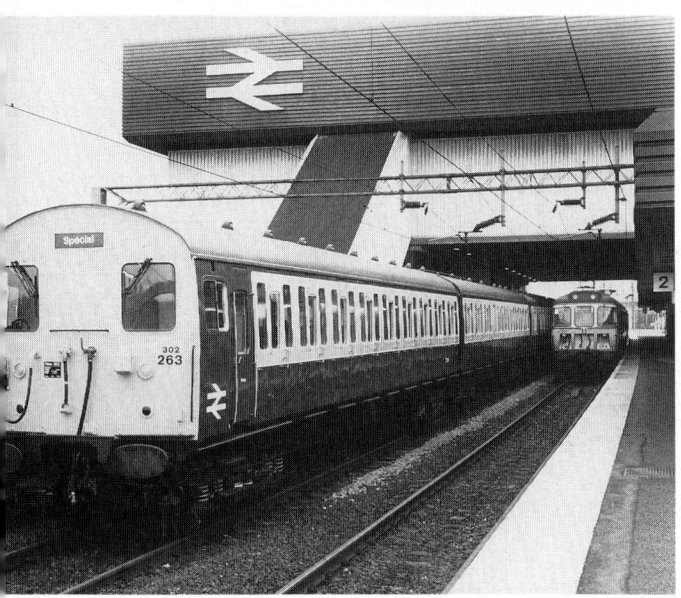

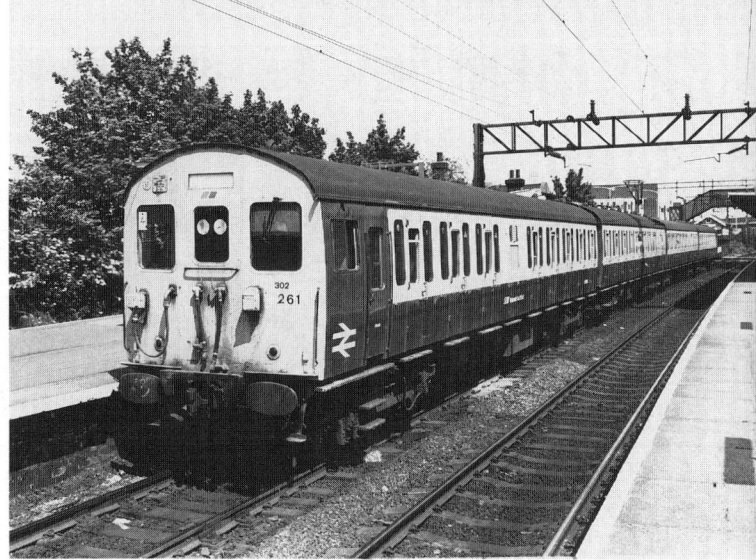

5 Pressed Steel, Paisley, ScR Glasgow Suburban Services, Class 303

Introduced: 1959
Purpose: North Clyde; Airdrie to Glasgow to Helensburgh services
South Clyde; Cathcart Circle
No of cars per unit: Three
Original unit numbers: 001-091
Present unit numbers: 303001-303091 (with gaps)
Equipment manufacturer: Metrovick
Traction motor type: MV 155 (four per unit)
Available horsepower: 828hp (155kW)
Maximum speed: 75mph (120km/hr)
Weight of unit: 129.20 tonnes
Length of unit: 58.36m (191ft 5½in)

The decision to electrify certain of the Glasgow suburban services provided one of the first opportunities for the BR Design Panel, created by the then British Transport Commission (BTC), to 'advise on the best means of obtaining a high standard of appearance and amenity in the design of its equipment' — such was its brief. No doubt pressures exerted by the ScR General Manager of the time also helped, and with the new trains to be built locally by the Pressed Steel Co Ltd of Linwood, Paisley, here was an opportunity to produce something worthy of the showpiece electrification scheme that was intended for Clydeside.

A full size 'above solebar' mock-up of a three-car unit was constructed at the Pressed Steel works, which enabled every external and internal detail of the design to be evaluated before the working drawings were produced. The livery was also evaluated, and it was to be a complete departure from the somewhat drab standard green of the period, the result being that a blue closely akin to that of the

Caledonian Railway returned once again to brighten the shores of the Clyde!

No less than 91 three-car units were ordered, of which 58 were intended for north side services and 33 for the south, and with passenger-operated powered sliding doors and spacious 3+2 seating in open saloons they were an instant success when public services commenced on North Clyde routes early in November 1960. There was obviously no comparison with the steam-hauled compartment stock trains which they had replaced, and with the tunnel sections now free of smoke those lucky enough to occupy the front seats could enjoy the excellent forward view afforded by the wrap-around windscreens. The publicity of the period capitalised on this feature particularly when the line ran close to the Clyde coast.

The first unit had been delivered in May 1959 and had undergone extensive trial running on the Styal line south of Manchester without trouble and, as parts of the line were energised, trial running and driver training commenced, and all looked well for the future. However, a series of transformer overheating failures occurred and one in particular, on 13 December 1960, culminated in an explosion and caused injury to seven passengers and the guard. The technical reasons for these are really outside the scope of this work, but it should perhaps be explained that although the main oil-cooled transformer is mounted on the underframe of the MBS vehicle, there is an equipment compartment located between the guard's compartment and the passenger saloon of that vehicle.

This compartment contained, as well as low-tension switchgear and other auxiliary

equipment, a reservoir and a conservator (header) tank for the transformer cooling oil and it was the formation of an explosive mixture of oil vapour and air in this compartment that caused the explosion.

Another explosion on 17 December brought about the cessation of all electric services, and on Monday 19 December steam services returned — this being a feat in itself since the steam depots had been closed and the locomotives and rolling stock had been dispersed.

The failures were the subject of two Ministry of Transport accident reports, which also covered problems which had beset the ER's LTSR units, and it was concluded that all the trains would need major modifications. The 77 MBS vehicles that had been delivered were sent to Manchester for modification by Metrovick, carried out in the former GCR Dukinfield works, whilst the remaining 14 vehicles

Below:
The drawing shows the BDTS vehicle of a non-refurbished Class 303 unit, ie with no access from the driving compartment to the passenger saloon and no inter-unit gangway connection. With this provision, and 2+2 seating, the seating capacity is considerably reduced from the 83 shown here to 56 for most of the refurbished vehicles. It is interesting to note that other first generation EMU trains have a cross vestibule immediately behind the driving compartment for the exclusive use of the driver, with inwards-opening slam doors to enable him to alight from the train in relative safety at, say, a lineside signal. These trains, and their later companions, have no such luxury and the driver has an *outwards-opening* slam door direct from the driving compartment which is, of course, somewhat out of gauge when open, and the driver must be alert to the passage of other trains on multi-track lines!
BR

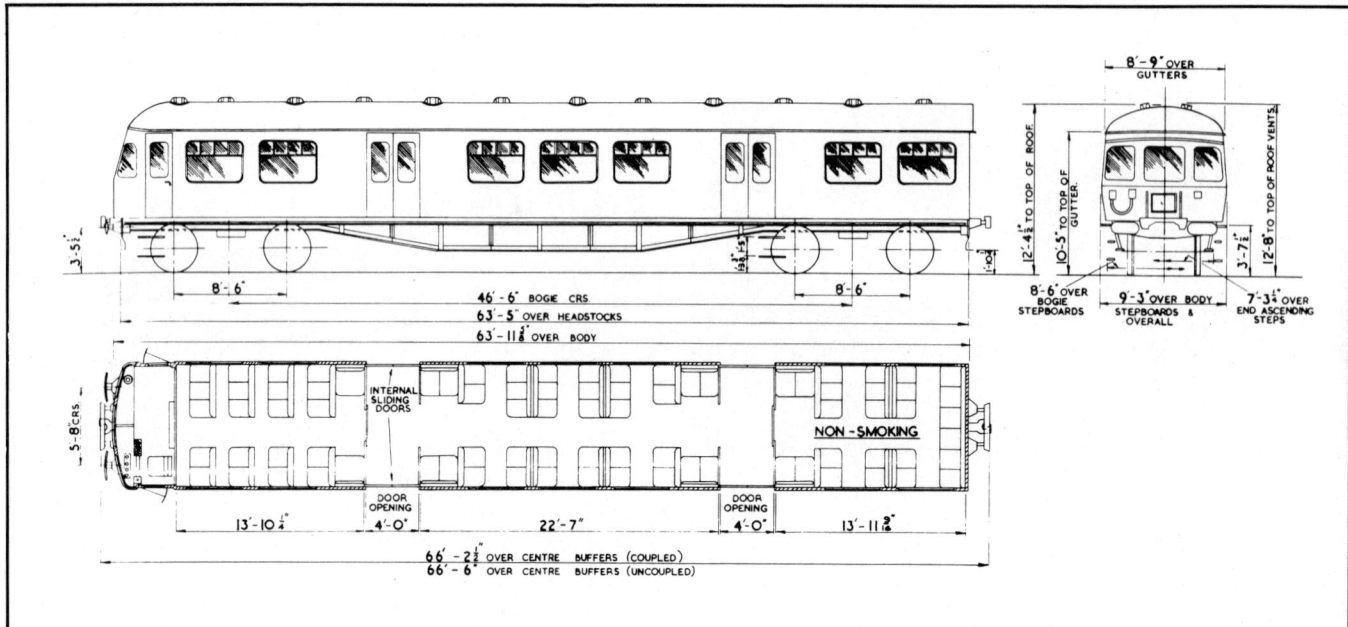

Above:
A Glasgow 'Blue Train' in all its splendour waits to depart from Helensburgh with a service for Airdrie via Singer on 26 May 1962. At this time no unit numbers were displayed, but the leading vehicle, No SC75823, relates to unit No 057 which heads this six-car train. *Brian Haresnape*

Left:
The wrap-around windscreens proved troublesome to keep watertight, and were difficult and expensive to replace, so a smaller flat screen was provided which slightly reduced the driver's sideways vision. Class 303 unit No 303057 has this modification and is shown at Crewe on 25 July 1983 working the stopping service to Manchester following its transfer to Longsight depot. An additional destination indicator has been provided but only the newer, lower position is used on LMR services. *Alec Swain*

were dealt with at Paisley before final delivery.

As soon as the first modified unit was available in March 1961 it was subjected to tests on the Styal line and, as others became available, each was tested on all the Glasgow lines from May onwards. Eventually the Inspecting Officer of the Ministry of Transport was satisfied and the electric service resumed on Sunday 1 October 1961 — no doubt to the relief of all those who had been involved!

Whilst all this had been taking place, work on the South Clyde network continued but the public opening was delayed by the need to modify the units, and this did not take place until May 1962, by which time Motherwell had been added to the network.

As built the trains were not gangwayed within the unit, and an initial refurbishment programme applied to units Nos 303083 and 303091 did not include such features, meaning that these two remain non-standard so far as seating capacity is concerned. The programme was soon amended to meet the requirements of driver-only operation, and the fitting of inter-vehicle gangways and the provision of a door from the driving compartment into the passenger saloon together with re-seating to 2+2 layout has considerably reduced the seating capacity. Nevertheless the 'Blue Trains' continue to serve Glasgow well, albeit mostly garbed in Strathclyde PTE orange and black livery after having carried the former 'Inter-City' BR medium blue and pale grey!

As mentioned in Section 2, 12 units were transferred to Manchester to work the Glossop and Hadfield services in particular, but may be seen elsewhere. They arrived in a variety of liveries but all have now gained the Greater Manchester PTE orange and brown scheme, yet remain in unrefurbished condition.

The future of the remaining unrefurbished units is bleak and those allocated to the ScR are liable to be withdrawn, together with their Class 311 counterparts, when the 22 new three-car Class 320 units are delivered from BREL York in 1990.

Details of Class 303: Built Pressed Steel 1959-61

DTS	19.50×2.82m	34.4t	56S	
MBS	19.36×2.82m	56.4t	48S	} all Gresley bogies
BDTS	19.50×2.82m	38.4t	56S	

Sets numbered 303001-303091 with gaps

DTS	numbered	75566-75600
		75746-75801
MBS	numbered	61481-61514*
		61812-61867*
BDTS	numbered	75601-75635
		75802-75857

* MBS has four MV 155kW motors

Note that unit withdrawals and reformations have led to some changes to the original numerical allocation of vehicles to units.

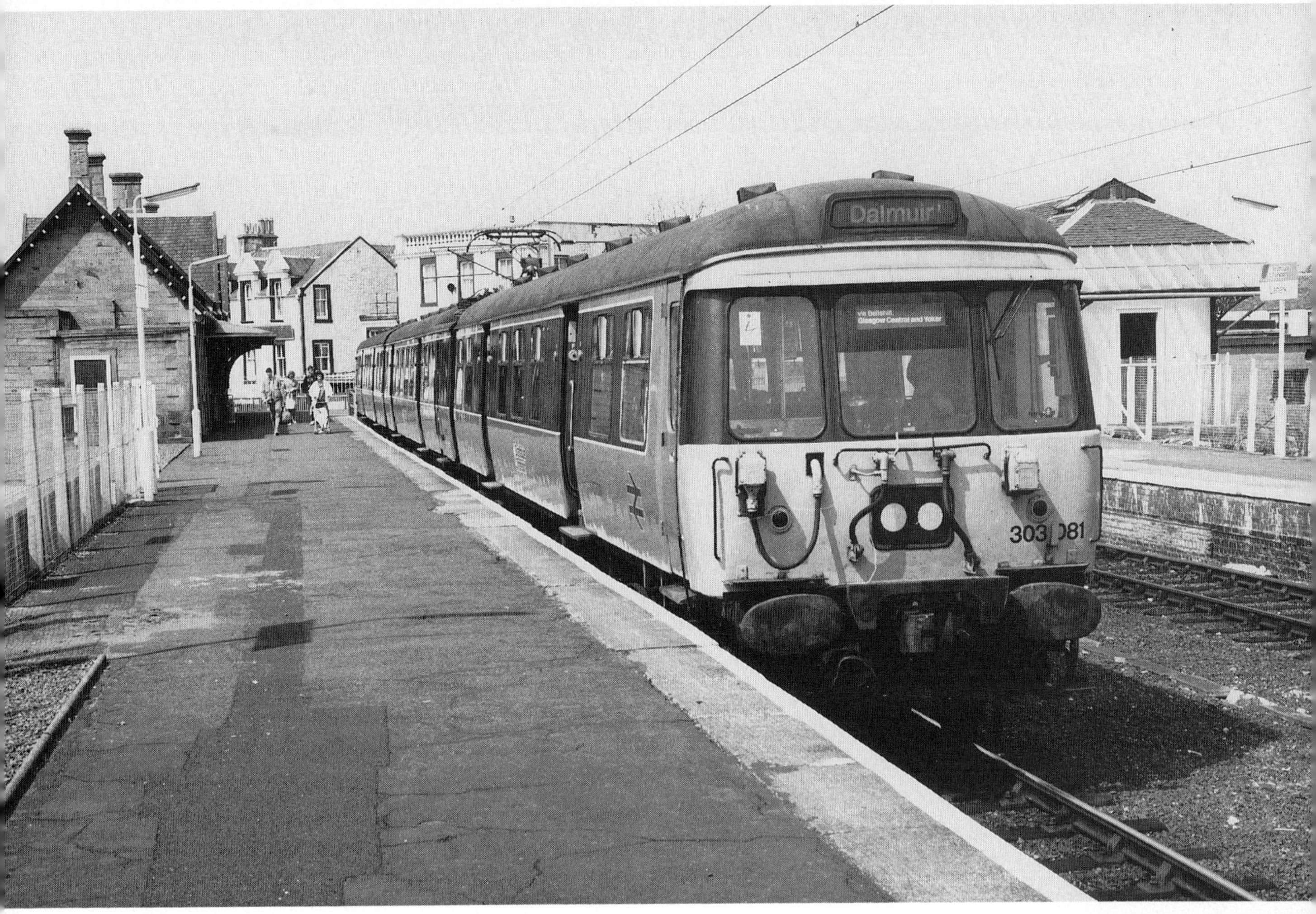
Dalmuir
303 081

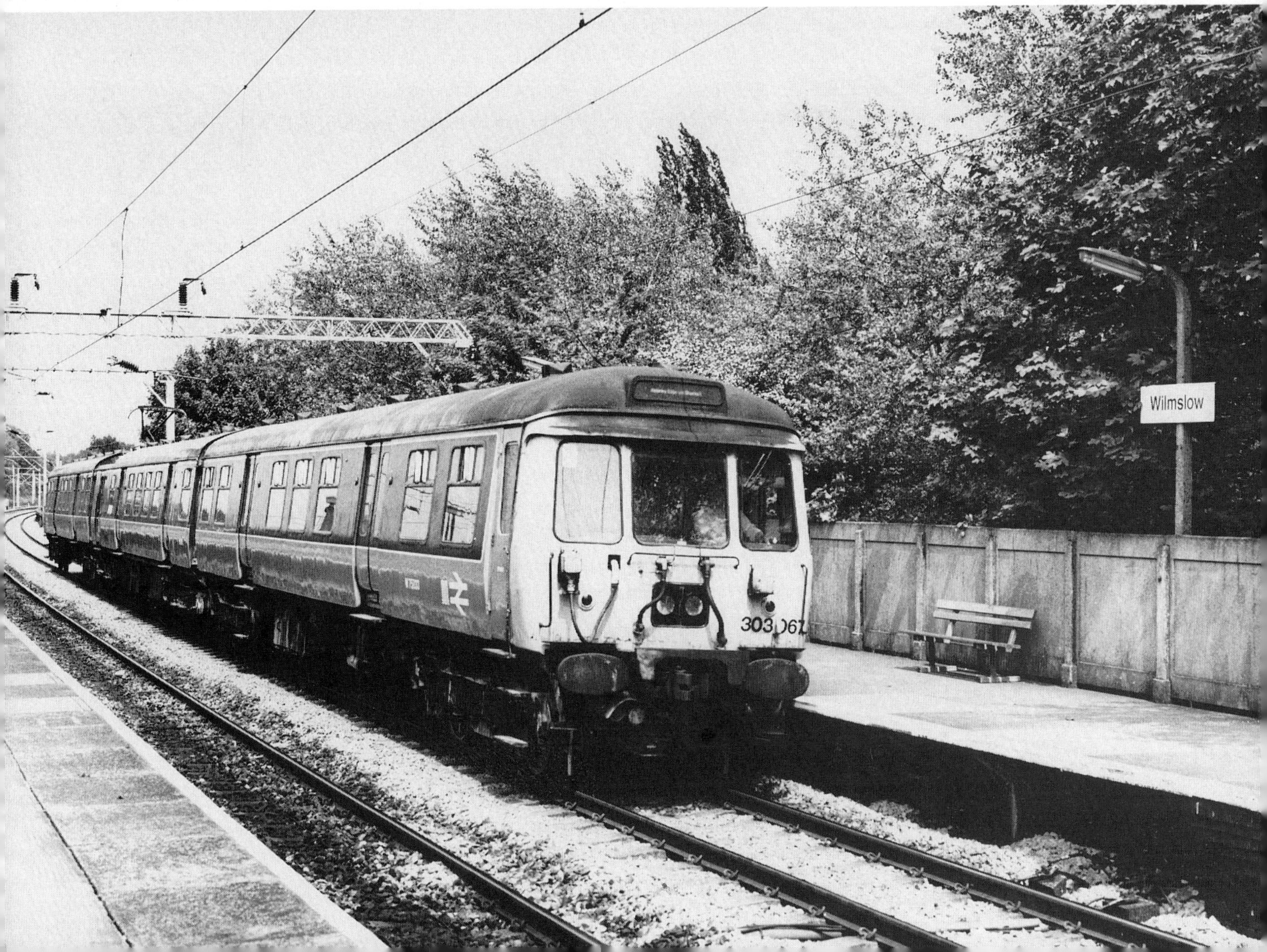
Wilmslow
303 067

6 BR Wolverton, LMR Main Line Stopping Services, Class 304

Introduced: 1960
Purpose: Crewe to Manchester/Liverpool/Stafford
No of cars per unit: Four (now reduced to three)
Original unit numbers: 001-045
Present unit numbers: 304001-304045 (with gaps)
Equipment manufacturer: BTH
Traction motor type: BTH (four per unit)
Available horsepower: 828hp (155kW)
Maximum speed: 75mph (120km/hr)
Weight of unit: 123.8 tonnes
Length of unit: 58.42m (191ft 11½in)

The events leading up to the electrification of the WCML have been chronicled in Part 6 of this series and need not be repeated here, but to provide the all-stations service between Crewe and Manchester the first of 15 'AM4' four-car units was delivered in April 1960 and undertook test running on the Styal line. The influence of the BR Design Panel could be seen in that the front end became much more stylish, a full-size mock-up of the front end being produced at Wolverton works to enable the design to be evaluated.

A further 21 units were built in 1961 for the Crewe to Liverpool service, which commenced on 1 January 1962, followed by a further nine in 1962 for the Crewe to Stafford section. The first units, now designated Class 304/1, had a compartment-type window and door layout despite the fact that, apart from the MBS vehicle, the accommodation was in open saloons. It was no doubt due to the Design Panel that the final 30 units (now Class 304/2) appeared with an all-saloon layout and much larger side windows which in fact spanned the seat backs, thus giving the interior a more spacious appearance. In recent years all the units have been refurbished, although they remain non-gangwayed, and are now reduced to a three-car formation, BDTS-MBS-DTBS, as there was no longer considered to be a requirement for first class accommodation, the spare TC vehicles being condemned and sold for scrap to a specialist dealer since they contained the now-unacceptable blue asbestos insulation. Thus the cost of refurbishment was reduced and the

Details of Class 304: Built Wolverton 1960/61				
BDTS	19.53×2.82m	36.8t	80S	
MBS	19.36×2.82m	54.5t	72S	} all Gresley bogies
DTBS	19.53×2.82m	32.5t	82S	

Sets numbered 304001-304045 with gaps

BDTS	numbered	75045-75059
		75680-75699
		75868-75877
MBS	numbered	61045-61059*
		61628-61647*
		61873-61882*
DTBS	numbered	75645-75679
		75858-75867

* MBS has four BTH 155kW motors

Note that despite unit withdrawals the original numerical allocation of vehicles to units has been maintained.

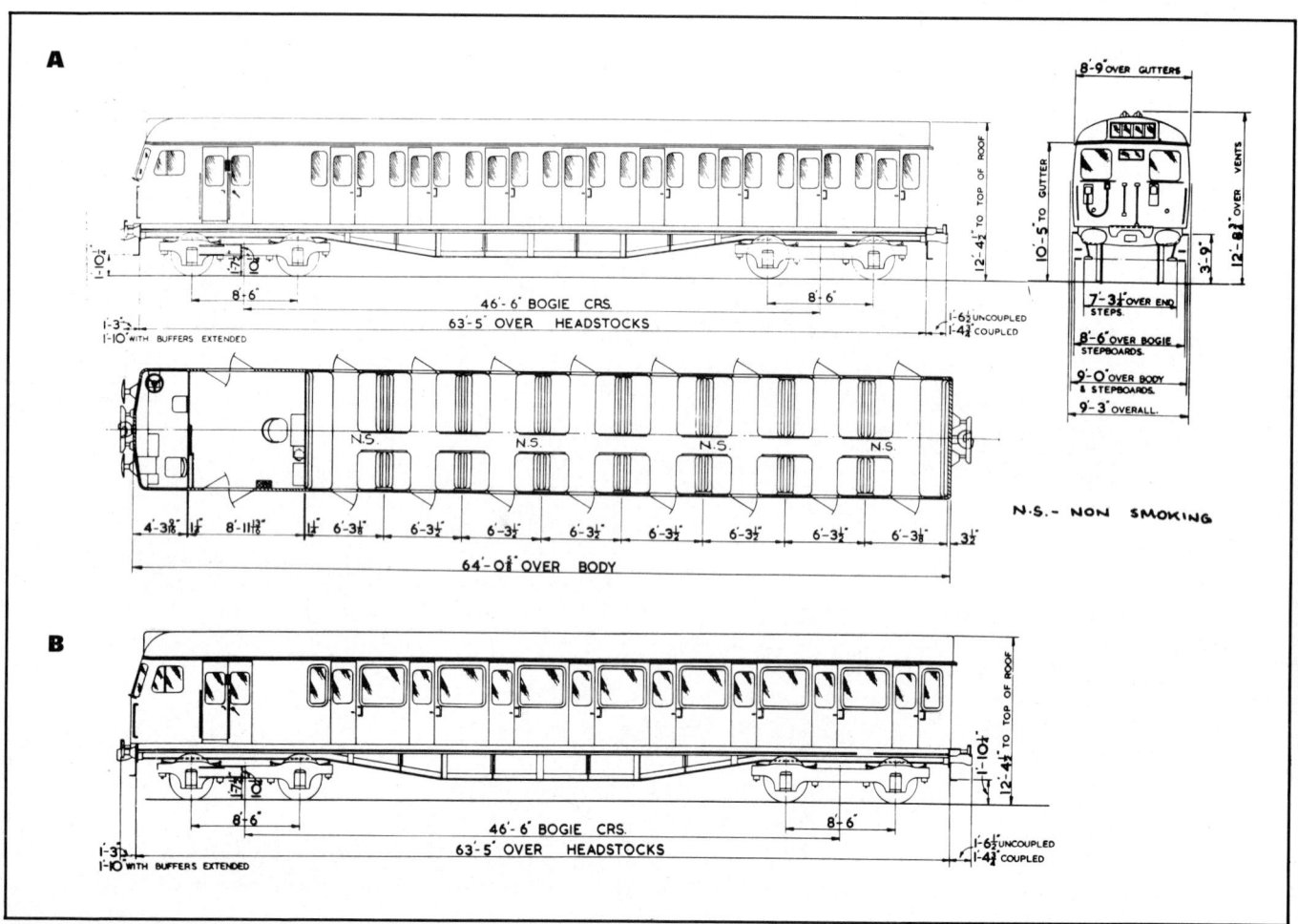

changed power/weight ratio produced an improved performance. The Class 304/1 MBS vehicles were at the same time converted to 3+2 open saloon seating to match the remaining vehicles.

They have remained allocated to Longsight depot and are still used on the services for which they were built, although several units have either been withdrawn entirely and sold for scrap due to changes in traffic requirements, or disbanded as the result of accident damage.

Left:
The alteration to the window layout, which took place after the first 15 units had been delivered, is clearly shown by these drawings of the DTBS vehicles of (A) Class 304/1 and (B) Class 304/2, related to the common open saloon seating layout. *BR*

Above:
'AM4' unit No 028 in lined green livery at Crewe in August 1961, showing the larger windows which exposed the seat backs. The DTBS vehicle is nearest the camera and the driver gains access to the driving compartment through the guard's compartment; therefore no cross vestibule is needed here. *Brian Haresnape*

Right:
Another 'AM4' unit, No 037 in lined green livery but with the addition of a small yellow warning panel, approaches Watford Junction on the up slow line on 22 September 1964. The headcode 3Z23 denotes a special empty stock movement, in this case a driver training run in preparation for the introduction of the 'AM10' units. In recent years the Class 304s have seldom worked south of Rugby. *BR*

Left:
Now in plain blue livery with full yellow ends, Class 304 unit No 009 calls at Adlington with the 13.25 Macclesfield-Manchester Piccadilly on 15 March 1980. The unit is still in four-car formation with the TC vehicle indicated by the yellow stripe above the first class accommodation. The black surround to the destination indicator seems to have been crudely applied. *Keith Smith*

Below:
Class 304 unit No 002 enters the now-lengthened MSJA platforms at Manchester Piccadilly on 22 May 1989 with an Altrincham via Stockport local service. Note that the class prefix is not carried by DTBS vehicle No M75646 of this now three-car formation. Class 90 locomotive No 90016 is alongside.
Alec Swain

Introduced: 1960
Purpose: Liverpool Street to Chingford/Enfield/Bishop's Stortford
No of cars per unit: Three (Class 305/1) or four (Class 305/2)
Original unit numbers: 401-455, 501-519
Present unit numbers: 305401-422
305501-528
Equipment manufacturer: GEC
Traction motor type: WT380 (four per unit)
Available horsepower: 820hp (612kW)
Maximum speed: 75mph (120km/hr)
Weight of unit: *305/1* 122.7 tonnes
305/2 157.2 tonnes
Length of unit: *305/1* 60.807m (199ft 6in),
305/2 80.975m (265ft 8in)

For the opening of the Liverpool Street to Chingford and Enfield services in November 1960 a total of 52 'AM5' (Class 305/1) three-car units were built at York, followed by a further three in 1962 — all to the same general design as the Crewe to Manchester/Liverpool stock and formed BDTS-MBS-DTS. For the outer-suburban services to Hertford and Bishop's Stortford, which were inaugurated at the same time, some first class and toilet accommodation was necessary; therefore York and Doncaster built 19 four-car units (Class 305/2) formed BDTC-MBS-TS-DTS.

In 1983 a programme of partial refurbishment, sometimes known as facelifting, commenced and further Class 305/2 units have been created by adding an additional vehicle to those of Class 305/1, which has created yet another formation variant, ie BDTS-MBS-TC-DTS and, for the first

Below:
The drawing shows the BDTS vehicle of a Class 305/2 unit before refurbishment, with the twin toilet compartments to suit the outer suburban work to Hertford and Bishop's Stortford for which they were built. *BR*

time, these later Class 305/2 units are now gangwayed within the unit and numbered 305521 onwards.

In 1984 a three-car Departmental unit, No 305935, was converted into a mobile classroom, the DT vehicles becoming classrooms and the MB a cinema. This has recently been refurbished and painted into InterCity livery to provide a mobile training unit for, initially, the ECML

electrification where a large number of maintenance staff require a special course in safe working on or near the overhead line equipment. The vehicles have been renumbered in the ADB Departmental series, and to replace one of the Class 305 DT vehicles (No 75496, which contained blue asbestos) vehicle No 75214 from disbanded Class 302 unit No 241 has been provided, thus forming a hybrid set.

Details of Class 305/1: Built York 1960

BDTS	19.53×2.82m	34.9t	92S	
MBS	19.36×2.82m	56.5t	72S	all Gresley bogies
DTS	19.53×2.82m	31.5t	92S	

Sets numbered 305401-305422

BDTS	numbered	75462-75482
		75506-75513
MBS	numbered	61429-61449* with gaps
		61473-61480*
DTS	numbered	75514-75534
		75558-75565

* MBS has four GEC WT380 153kW motors

Class 305/2: Built York/Doncaster 1960

BDTC	19.53×2.82m	36.5t	24F	52S	
BDTS*	19.53×2.82m	34.9t		92S	
MBS	19.36×2.82m	56.5t		76S	all Gresley bogies
TS	19.36×2.82m	31.5t		86S	
TC*	19.36×2.82m	31.0t	19F	60S	
DTS	19.53×2.82m	32.7t		88S	

Sets numbered 305501-305519

* 305521-305528 reformed from Class 305/1

BDTC	numbered	75424-75442
BDTS	numbered	75464-75512
MBS	numbered	61410-61428*
		61431-61479* with gaps
TS	numbered	70356-70374
TC	numbered	70093-70645
DTS	numbered	75443-75461
		75516-75564

* MBS has four GEC WT380 153kW motors

Note that unit withdrawals and reformations have meant that the numerical allocation of vehicles has not been strictly maintained, particularly the TC vehicles of units Nos 305521 onwards, which are being formed from three-car Class 305/1s.

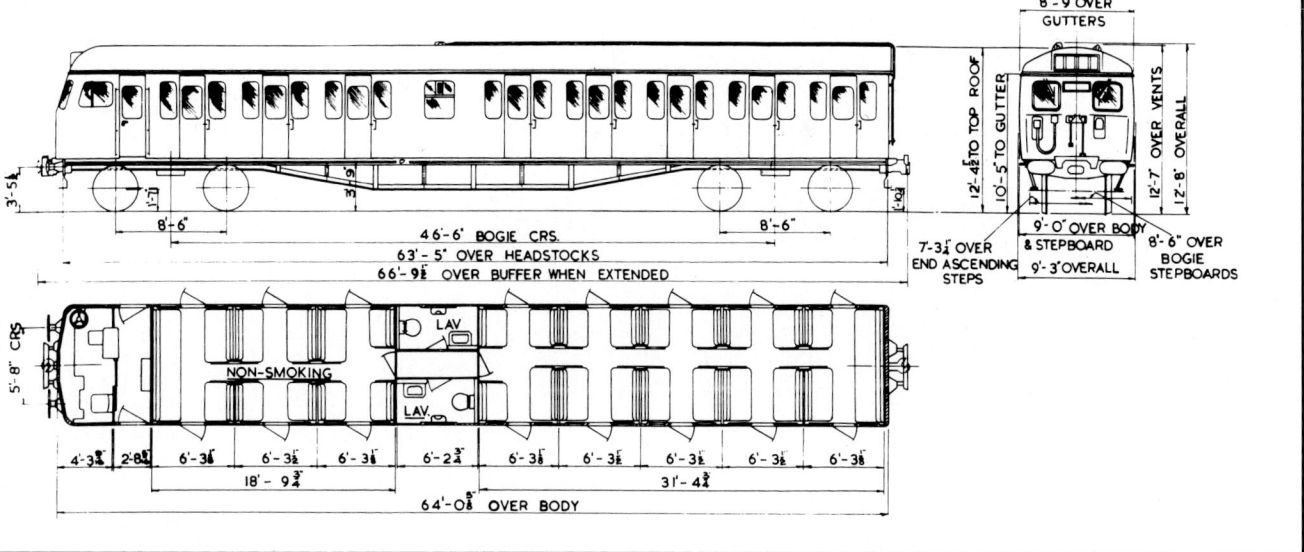

Above left:
A train of two three-car 'AMS' units, as they were then known, between Rye House and Hertford on 2 June 1960 during trial running prior to their introduction in November of that year. Their plain green livery, without even the yellow line at waist level, was a little disappointing after the work of the Design Panel in improving the front end appearance. DTS No E75530 is the leading vehicle of unit No 417. *BR*

Left:
A change to blue livery does little to enhance the appearance of Class 305/2 unit No 515 leaving Southend Victoria with the 11.45 to Liverpool Street on 12 September 1976, although the full yellow end and white blanks in the route indicator do enliven the front end when compared with the previous photograph. *Brian Morrison*

Above:
A rural scene at St Margaret's, once the junction for Buntingford, as Class 305/1 unit No 422 in blue/grey livery calls with a train for Hertford East on 26 September 1982. *John C. Baker*

Right:
An unusual task for Class 305 unit No 305439, seen here passing Bescot being propelled by Class 87/1 No 87101 on 25 March 1986. These runs were early trials to establish the feasibility of modern push-pull operation which has led to the driving van trailer concept which is today being introduced on the West Coast and East Coast main lines. Note the alteration to the jumper cable arrangements and the extensions to the main reservoir and brake pipe hoses which run along the underframes of the vehicles. *C. J. Tuffs*

Introduced: 1961
Purpose: Liverpool Street to Shenfield/Southend services
No of cars per unit: Three or four
Original unit numbers:
133-165, 313-321, 453-455
Present unit numbers:
308133-308165 (308/1)
308991-308995 (308/2)
Equipment manufacturer: English Electric
Traction motor type: EE 536A (four per unit)
Available horsepower: 770hp (574kW)
Maximum speed: 75mph (120km/hr)
Weight of unit: 119.8 or 155.5 tonnes
Length of unit: 60.808m (199ft 6in) or 80.975m (265ft 8in)

These trains, built at York, were originally known as the Southend Augumentation Stock, but over the years have appeared, as Class 308/1, on most of the GE lines services and have become, like many others, 'common user'. Subjected to the now-standard programme of refurbishment, they are presently gangwayed within the unit, but over the years they have been involved in a number of reformations resulting, at one time, in no less than four sub-classes, ie 308/1, 308/2, 308/3 and 308/4!

The Class 308/2 units are unique, and were built for the Tilbury line services where there remained some special traffic, including that emanating from the cruise liners which called at Tilbury. This traffic required a larger area of luggage accom-

Details of Class 308/1: Built York/Doncaster 1961

BDTC	19.53×2.82m	36.3t	24F	52S	
MBS	19.36×2.82m	55.0t		76S	all Gresley bogies
TS	19.36×2.82m	31.4t		86S	
DTS	19.53×2.82m	33.0t		88S	

Sets numbered 308133-308165

BDTC numbered 75878-75886
75896-75919
MBS numbered 61883-61915*
TS   numbered 70611-70643
DTS numbered 75887-75895
75929-75952

* MBS has four EE536A 143.5kW motors

Class 308/2: Built York 1961

BDTS	19.53×2.82m	34.8t	80S	
MLV	19.35×2.82m	54.0t	—	all Gresley bogies
DTLV	19.53×2.82m	31.0t	—	

Sets numbered 308991-308995

BDTS numbered 75924-75928
MLV numbered 68012-68018*
DTLV numbered 75957-75961

* MLV has four EE536A 143.5kW motors

Note that on the four remaining units the MLV vehicles are no longer allocated in numerical sequence.

modation to be provided and therefore the motor coach was entirely devoted to this purpose. Hence these trains were formed BDTS-MLV-TC-DTS, with the MLV vehicle containing portable tables, cycle hooks, lift-up shelves and even a fish stowage area! They were converted to three-car formation in 1984 by removal of the TC and DTS vehicles, the latter being replaced by a DTLV converted from Class 308/3 DTS vehicles and were to be found working for the Parcels Sector into 1989, having taken the place of locomotive-hauled parcels trains. However, their role has now been taken over by the Class 302 conversions referred to in Section 4.

Below:
Since the layout of the majority of vehicles contained within Class 308 units conform to those previously described, the opportunity has been taken to include this drawing of the unique MLV vehicles which are formed within sub-class 308/2 units. *BR*

Above right:
An official photograph of MLV No E68011. The large board on the ground reads '1961 Carriage Building Programme Augmented GE Suburban Service Rolling Stock Construction Order CMEE 179'. The inside-spring bogies make an interesting comparison with those of the LYR Holcombe Brook vehicles. *BR*

Right:
Class 308/2 parcels unit No 308994 passes Stratford on 30 December 1985, soon to be overtaken by a Class 86 locomotive on a Norwich train. *Michael J. Collins*

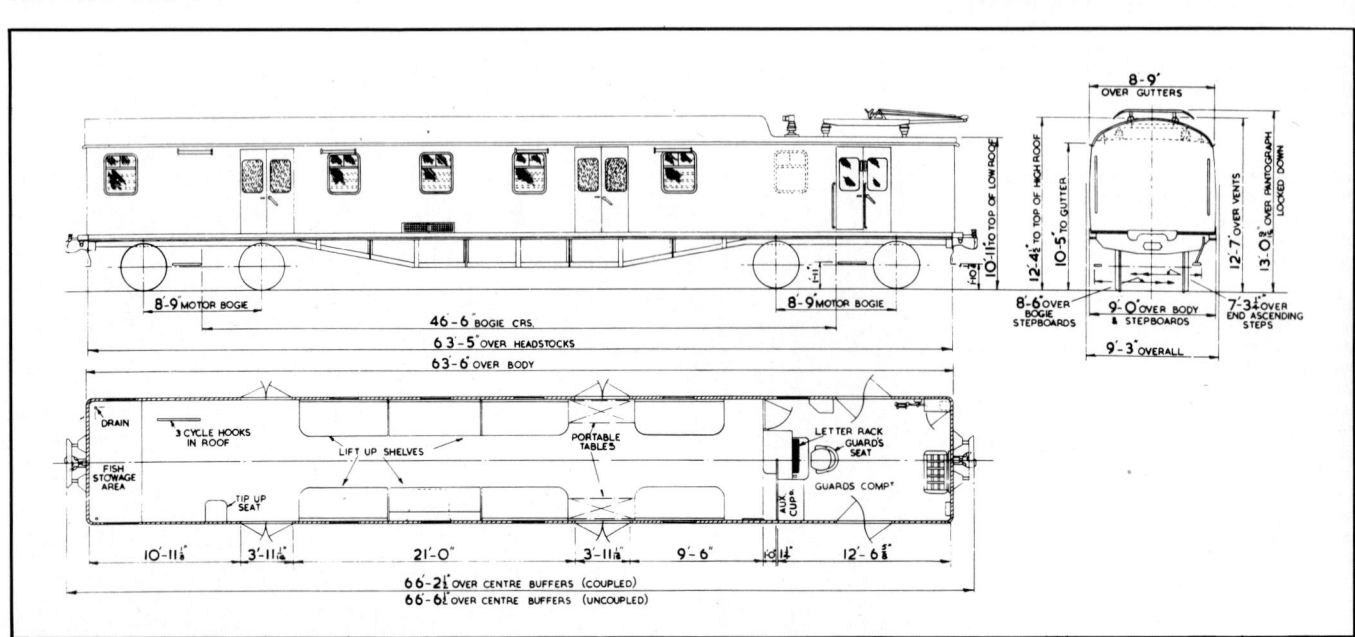

1961 CARRIAGE BUILDING PROGRAMME
AUGMENTED G.E. SUBURBAN SERVICE
ROLLING STOCK CONSTRUCTION ORDER
C.M.E.E.179

Above:
Class 308/1 unit No 144 in blue livery heads a Colchester to Ilford ECS working, passing Marks Tey on 23 July 1980. The branch to Sudbury diverges to the left. *Michael J. Collins*

Below:
Class 308/1 unit No 308143 in blue/grey livery calls at Grays with an Upminster to Tilbury Riverside service on 27 May 1989; such units now form the bulk of the trains to that terminus. *Alec Swain*

Introduced: 1962
Purpose: Liverpool Street to Clacton/Walton-on-Naze services
No of cars per unit: Two or four
Original unit numbers: 601-627
Present unit numbers: 309601-309608, 309611-309627 (with gaps)
Equipment manufacturer: GEC
Traction motor type: WT 401 (four per unit)
Available horsepower: 1,128hp (841kW)

Maximum speed: 100mph (160km/hr)
Weight of unit: *309/1* 170.5 tonnes,
309/2 169.1 tonnes
Length of unit: 80.975m (265ft 8in)

For the commencement of electric services to Clacton and Walton in March 1963 a build of eight two-car and 15 four-car 'AM9' units was ordered from York, to the general BR Mk 1 locomotive-hauled coach design but with rounded outer ends

Below:
The drawings depict (A) the DMBS vehicle of a Class 309/1 unit, where the pantograph is mounted close to the driving compartment and above the guard's compartment, and (B) the intermediate MBS vehicle of a Class 309/2 unit. Both show the refurbished condition with space for a catering trolley, a facility far removed from the griddle (buffet) car that eight of the units once had! *BR*

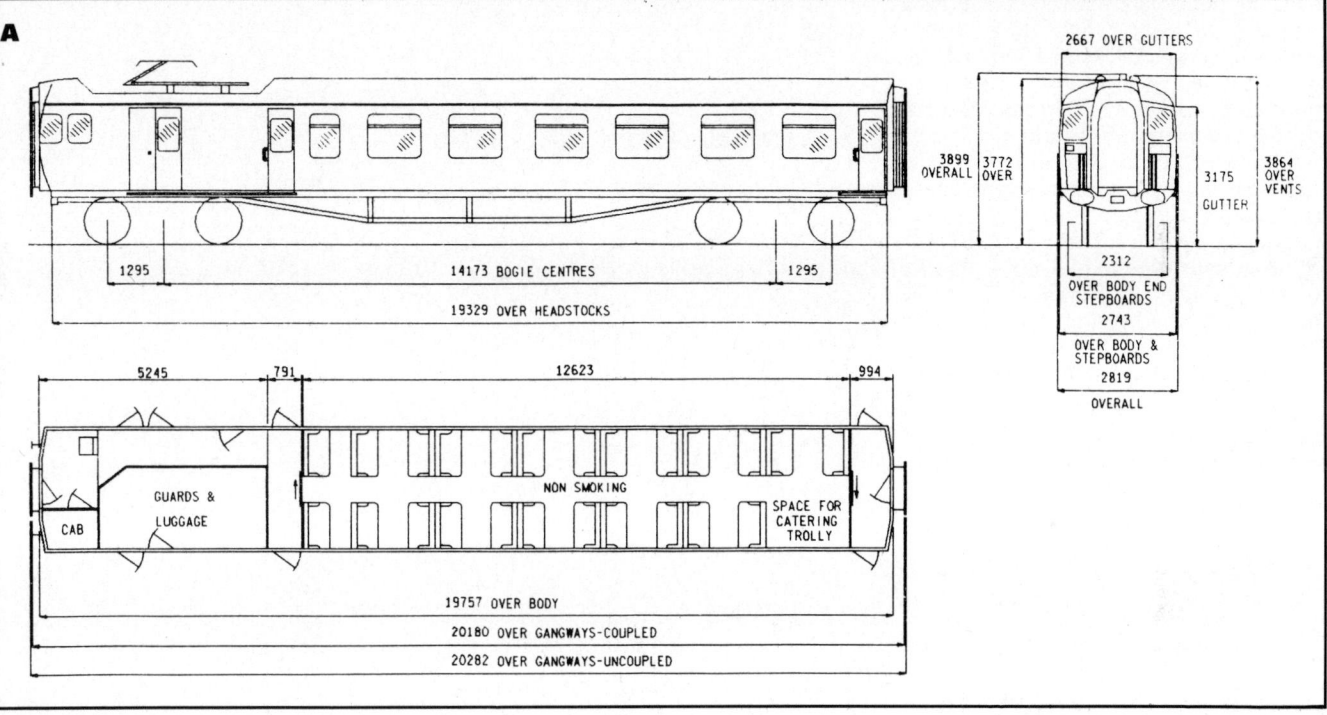

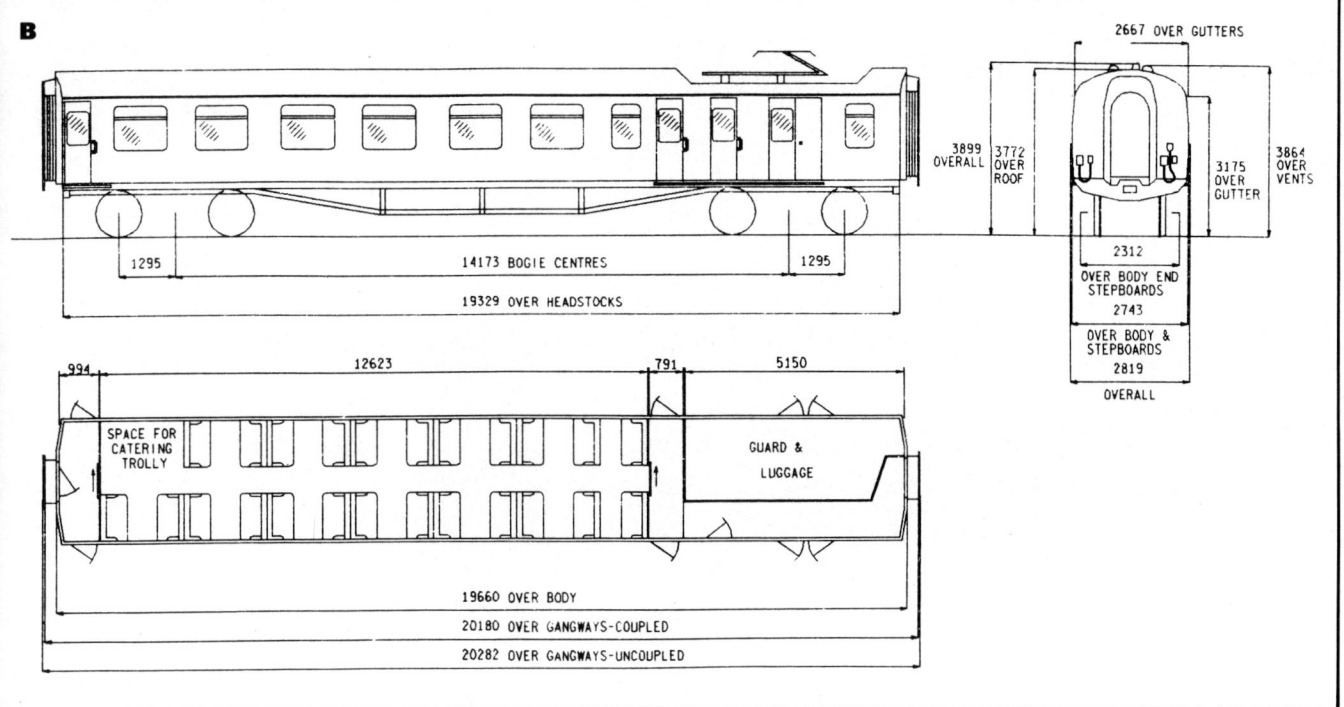

incorporating an inter-unit gangway connection. Painted in the then standard maroon livery with lining to denote their express status, they were for some years the only BR EMU train officially capable of 100mph running. Like their suburban compatriots they have been subjected to a number of reformations over the years, due to changed service patterns and catering requirements, and from 1985 onwards they have been refurbished with new seating, fluorescent lighting, public address and hopper ventilators.

These changes may perhaps best be explained by reference to the vehicle on which the pantograph is mounted, and relating this to their latter-day classification. Thus DMBS vehicles from the original two-car units have the pantograph mounted immediately above the driving compartment, and these now power Class 309/1, formed DMBS-TS-TC-BDTS. The additional vehicles were converted from Mk 1 coaches in 1973 (units Nos 605 to 608 becoming for a while sub-class 309/4) and 1981 (units Nos 601 to 604). The MBS vehicles, with the pantograph above the guard's compartment, now power Class 309/2, formed DTS-TS-MBS-BDTC. Of these units Nos 611 to 618 originally contained griddle (buffet) cars but these were removed and replaced by converted TS vehicles in 1981. The remaining units, Nos 621 to 627 (once sub-class 309/3), are

still formed as built, although refurbished to the general specification.

The rounded corners to the driving ends were initially provided with wrap-around windscreens, but problems with the ingress of water and the difficulty and expense of replacement has led to their replacement by two smaller panes in recent years.

A number of units were painted in the ex-London & South East Sector 'Jaffa Cake' livery of brown, beige and orange incorporating the legend 'Essex Express' but with recent overhauls all have now lost their 'express' status and have appeared in the standard Network SouthEast red white, blue and grey colours.

Details of Class 309/1: Built York/Wolverton 1962-81

DMBS	19.76×2.82m	60.2t		52S	
TS	19.67×2.82m	34.5t		64S	all Commonwealth bogies
TC	19.67×2.82m	35.6t	24F	28S	
BDTS	19.76×2.82m	40.2t		60S	

Sets numbered 309601-309608

DMBS numbered 61940-61947*
TS numbered 71569-71572
71107-71110†
TC numbered 71573-71576
71111/71114†
BDTS numbered 75984-75991

* DMBS has four GEC WT401 210kW motors.
† TS and TC vehicles not allocated to units in numerical sequence.

Class 309/2: Built York/Wolverton 1962-87

BDTC	19.76×2.82m	40.0t	18F	32S	
MBS	19.67×2.82m	57.7t		52S	all Commonwealth bogies
TS	19.67×2.82m	34.8t		68S	
DTS	19.76×2.82m	36.6t		56S	

Sets numbered 309611-309627 with gaps

BDTC numbered 75637-75644
75962-75968
MBS numbered 61925-61939*
TS numbered 71754-71761
70253-70259
DTS numbered 75976-75983
75969-75975

* MBS has four GEC WT401 210kW motors

Below:
In the lined maroon express livery of the day, 'AM9' unit No 627 heads a down Clacton and Walton service, calling at Witham on 5 October 1963. *Alec Swain*

Above:
**Buffet car No GE69103, photographed when
new on 8 August 1962. Changes in catering
requirements led to the complete withdrawal
of these cars in 1981 and the eight remaining
vehicles of the original nine were sold for
scrap in 1984 as no further use could be found
for them.** *BR*

Left:
**Although there were no brackets for the
traditional destination boards at roof level,
which had been perpetuated on the
locomotive-hauled Mk 1 stock, the 'AM9'
units had provision for small boards on a
central window pillar of each vehicle to
ensure that passengers boarded the correct
portion of the train. No doubt staff were
available in those days to change them at the
destination!** *BR*

Left:
The problems that had beset the wrap-around windscreens of the Class 303 and 311 units plagued the 309s as well, but it took several years for all to be modified. DMBS vehicle No E61946 of Class 309/1 set No 607 was still in original condition at Clacton on 11 March 1980, coupled to a modified example. *Alec Swain*

Below:
Class 309/2 buffet unit No 612 in blue/grey livery heads a down Clacton service climbing Brentwood Bank on 19 May 1977 and clearly shows the modified windscreen arrangements. *Brian Morrison*

Above right:
A refurbished Class 309/1 unit No 309605 in London & South East Sector livery of brown, beige and orange, complete with 'Essex Express' legend, stands at Walton-on-the-Naze having arrived with the 17.30 from Liverpool Street on 12 June 1985. Note the headlight now mounted in the recess for the brake pipe hoses and control jumper cable. This is a requirement for 100mph rolling stock. One wonders if a more pleasing effect could have been obtained by continuing the black windscreen surround to include the small side window as well, in much the same way as the Class 303 units. *Colin Boocock*

Below right:
Class 309/1 unit No 309605, in Network SouthEast livery, is formed at the rear of the 15.15 Liverpool Street-Clacton, seen leaving Shenfield on 17 June 1989. *Alec Swain*

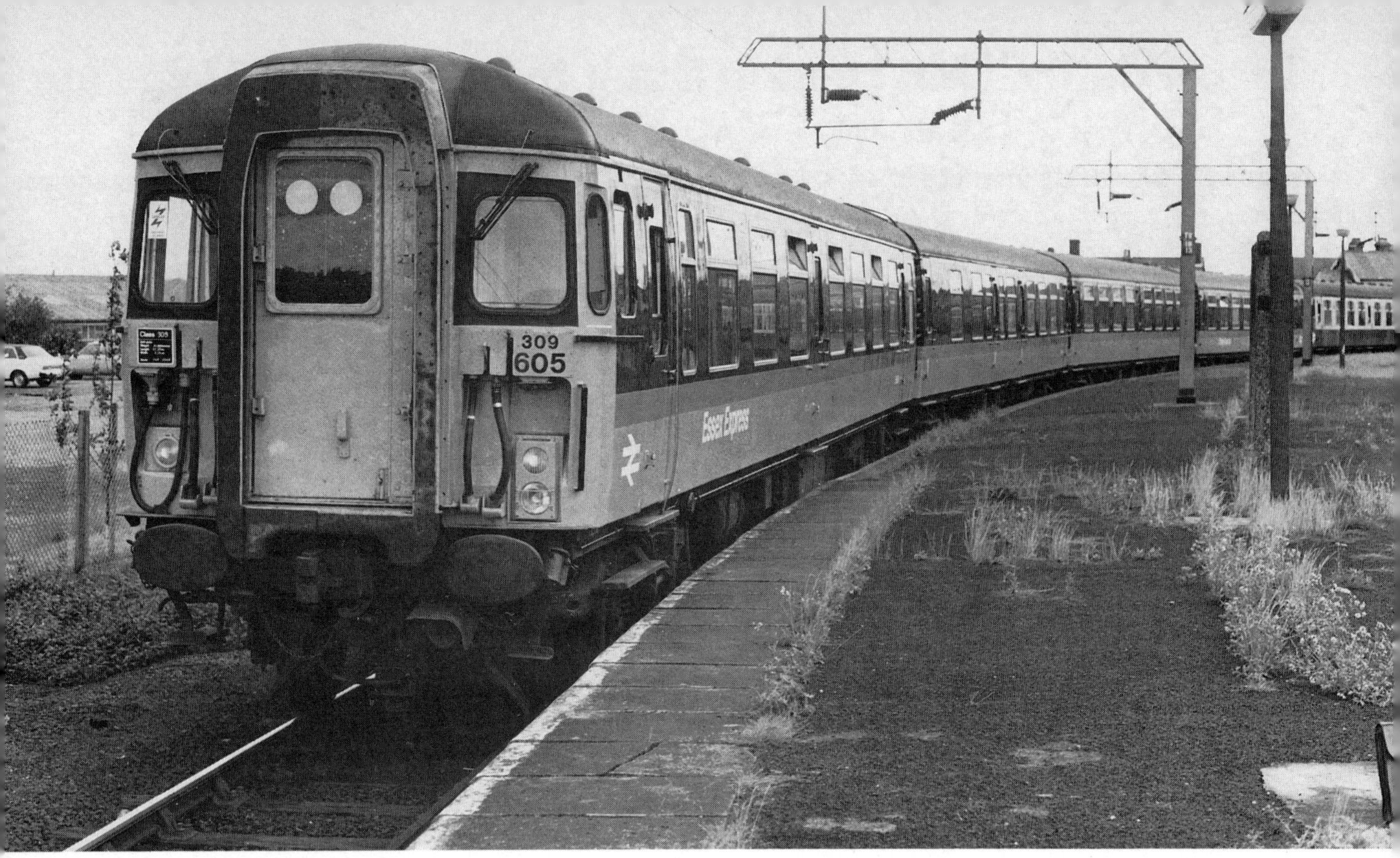
309
605
Essex Express

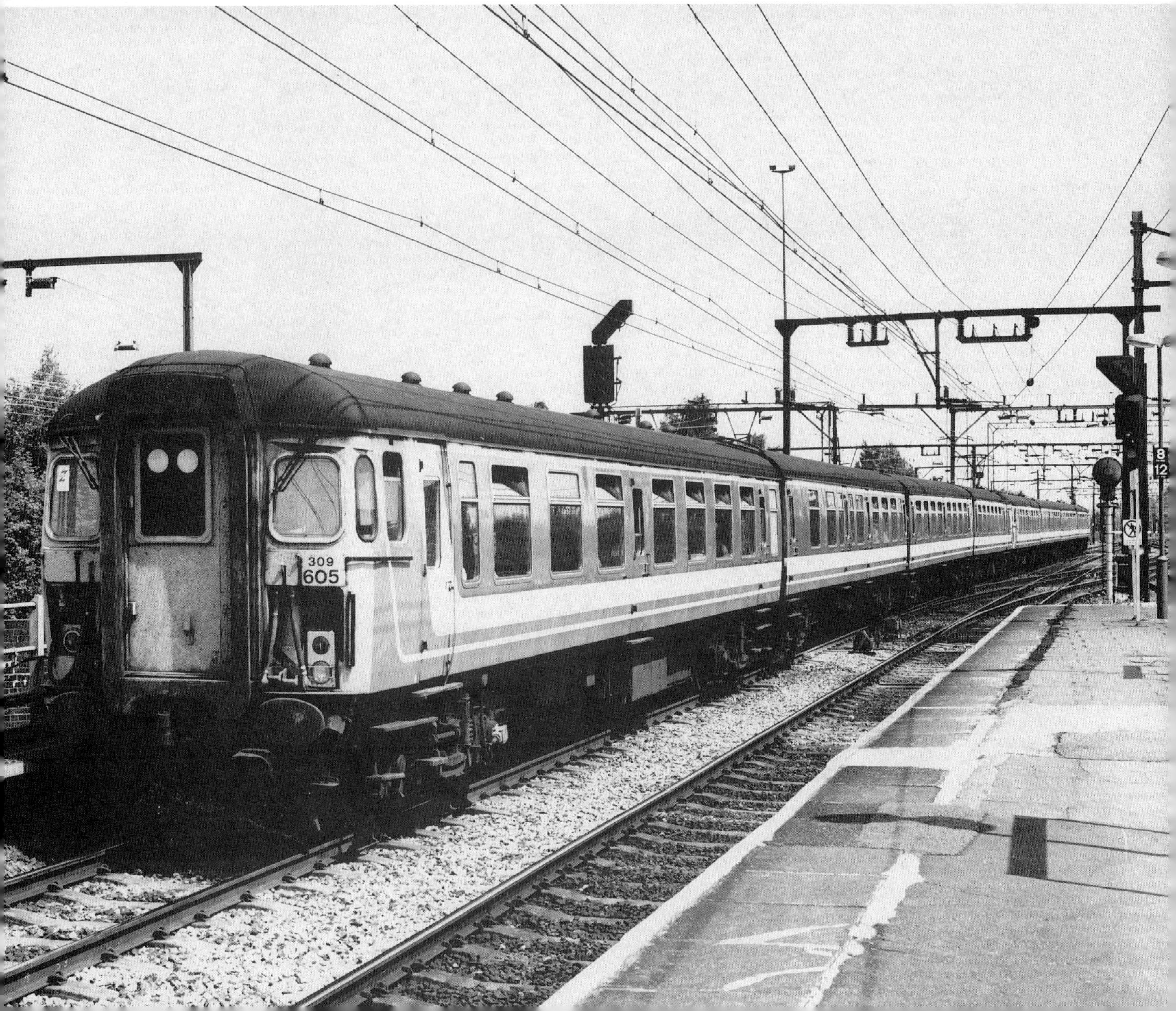
309
605
8
12

Introduced: 1965
Purpose: Euston to Northampton and Birmingham stopping services
No of cars per unit: Four
Original unit numbers: 046-095
Present unit numbers:
310046-310095 (310/0 with gaps)
310101-310111 (310/1)
Equipment manufacturer: English Electric
Traction motor type: EE 546A (four per unit)
Available horsepower: 1,080hp (806kW)
Maximum speed: 75mph (120km/hr)
Weight of unit: 160.60 tonnes
Length of unit: 80.975m (265ft 8in)

By the 1960s the Design Panel was having a decided influence on the appearance of new rolling stock, and the 50 'AM10' trains required for the Euston to Birmingham stopping services, to be built at Derby, were the first to appear in the standard all-blue multiple-unit livery. This was relieved by the aluminium window surrounds being left unpainted. Technically the vehicles were of integral construction, without the traditional underframe, and this allowed the underslung equipment to occupy the full width of the coach body. Considerable efforts were made to soundproof the passenger saloons and the provision of B4 bogies gave a good ride quality; indeed, a contemporary press report following a demonstration run between Watford and Tring speaks in glowing terms; 'even with door droplights and sliding window ventilators open, sound

Below:
The DTC vehicle of a Class 310 unit. Note that when built first class non-smokers had to pass through a potentially smoke-filled area to reach their accommodation! The function of the two areas has now been reversed. *BR*

levels did not rise appreciably. On welded track at full speed the trains glide without any appreciable unsteadiness, and it was possible to write easily even over motor coach bogies'.

They were the first multiple-unit trains to have the now-standard disc brakes, and of these the report said '[they] provide a far smoother deceleration than traditional brake blocks, but a demonstration of an emergency stop proved somewhat of an anti-climax for, although the train halted from 75mph in about 800yd in 33sec, the effect was less noticeable than a normal service stop by existing air-braked stock.' It is perhaps surprising that the presence of slam doors, on this otherwise modern stock, was not commented upon. However it was noted that, despite the provision of glazed partitions between the driving compartment and the passenger saloon 'only standing passengers are able to see forward or backward'. This was evidently before the blinds, intended for use during the hours of darkness, remained down all day!

The units, later to become Class 310, were formed in the standard fashion, ie BDTS-MBS-TS-DTC, but as built they were gangwayed between the outer pairs of vehicles only, ie one could not pass between the MBS and TS vehicles. This, however, was rectified on refurbishment in the interests of on-train revenue protection.

In common with other multiple-unit trains the blue/grey livery was applied from the late 1970s and the distinctive aluminium window surrounds were painted over, and with the advent of Network SouthEast the majority now carry that Sector's livery. In addition, many have been transferred to the ER and allocated to East Ham and Ilford depots, following the arrival of Class 317/1 units displaced from the St Pancras/Moorgate to Bedford line.

Once again the wrap-around windscreens have proved troublesome, for just the same reasons as those fitted to Classes 303, 309 and 311 and at overhaul smaller, flat panes are being provided.

Details of Class 310: Built Derby 1965-67

BDTS	19.86×2.82m	37.3t		80S	
MBS	19.93×2.82m	57.2t		70S	
TS	19.93×2.82m	31.7t		100S	all B4 bogies
DTC	19.86×2.82m	34.4t	25F	43S	
DTS#	19.86×2.82m	34.4t		68S	

Sets numbered 310046-310095 (Class 310/1) — with gaps
310101-310111 (Class 310/2#)

BDTC	numbered	76130-76179
MBS	numbered	62071-62120*
TS	numbered	70731-70780
DTC/DTS#	numbered	76180-76229

* MBS have four EE546 201.5kW motors

Note that reformations and vehicle replacement, together with the creation of sub-class 310/2 has broken the numerical sequence of allocation to units.

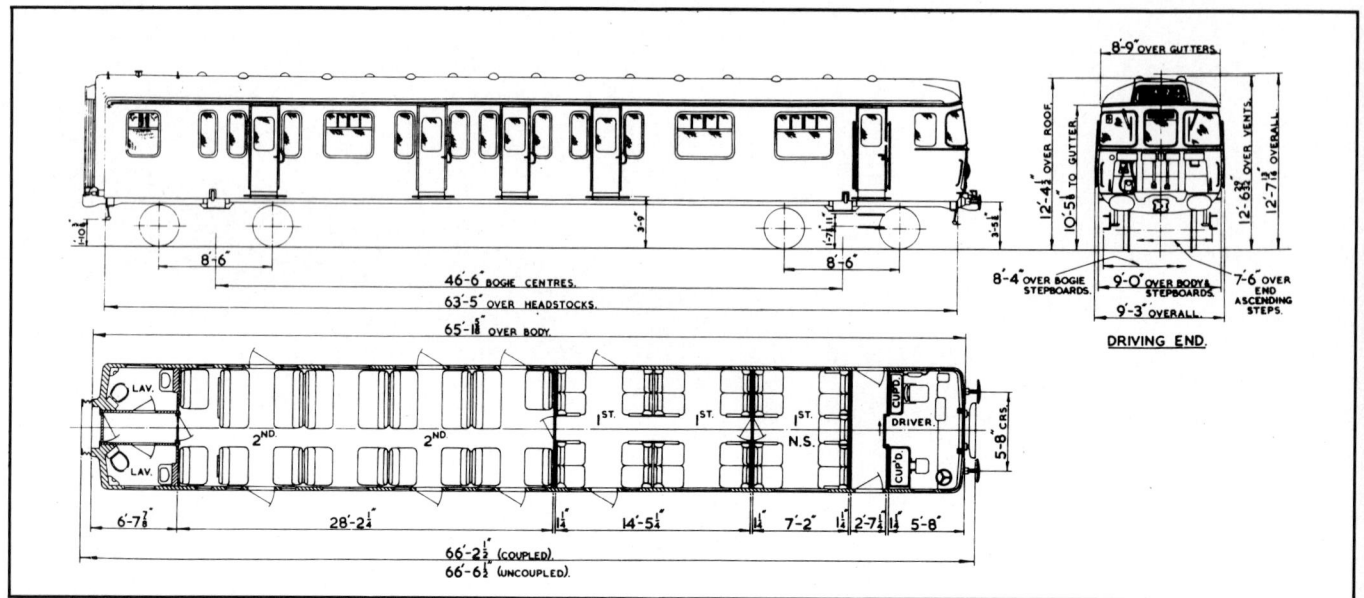

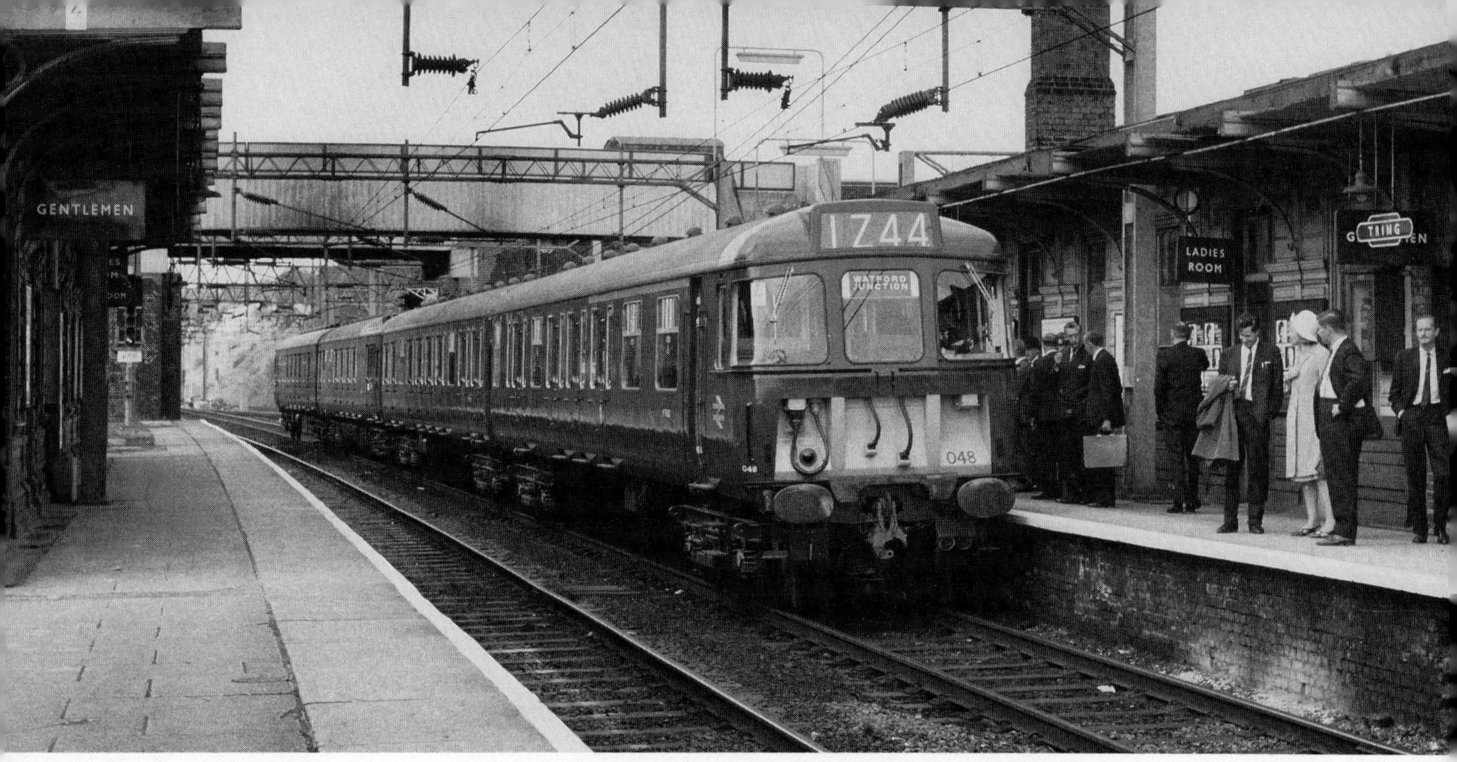

Above:
This photograph shows the press run from Watford to Tring in August 1965 which produced the favourable comments mentioned in the text. 'AM10' unit No 048 in blue livery with small yellow warning panel waits at Tring to return the party to Watford Junction. *Ian Allan Library*

Right:
An impressive view of 'AM10' unit No 047, showing the considerable visual improvement achieved by extending the yellow warning panel. *BR*

Below right:
With a full yellow end and in blue/grey livery, Class 310 unit No 310074 passes the site of the main line platforms at Willesden Junction on 21 July 1983 with a Euston-bound train. The cooling towers of Acton Lane power station dominate the background. *Alec Swain*

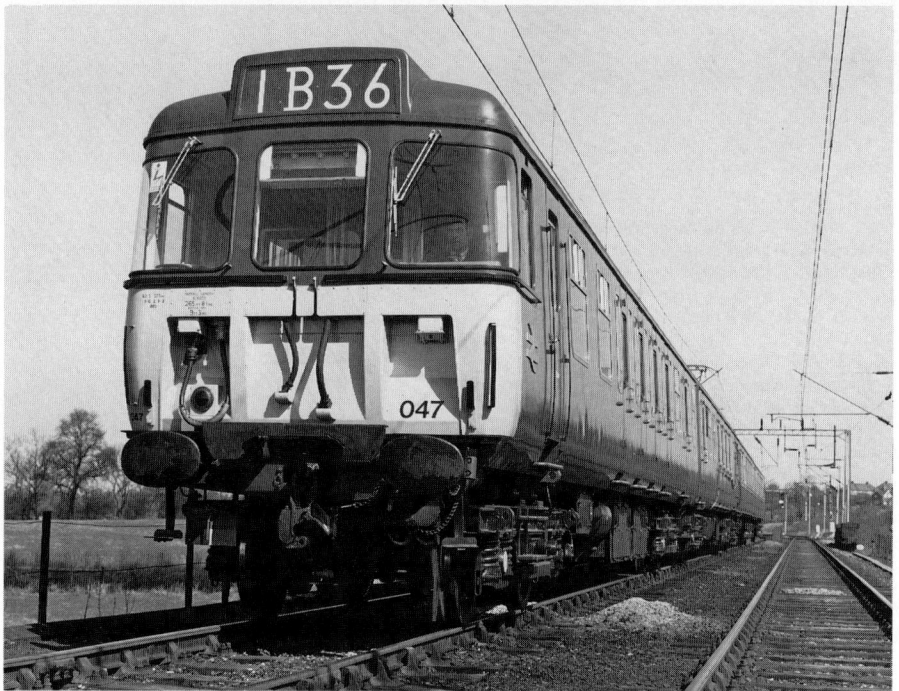

There have been a number of losses and reformations due to accident damage but mention must be made of BDTS vehicle No 76998 formed in unit No 094, which was rebuilt from TS No 70756, one of the survivors of an accident at Roade on the last day of December 1969 when formed in unit No 071.

A recent development has been the creation of a new sub-class, 310/1, for Provincial services, refurbished and painted in the grey, aircraft blue and light blue livery of that Sector, with the DTC vehicle declassified to DTS and seating 68. These are allocated to Bletchley depot and work in the West Midlands PTE area, having been renumbered 310101 onwards.

Finally, as a result of the increase in traffic on the Thameslink services, and pending the building of further Class 319 units, it has been necessary to return a number of Class 317/1 units to Cricklewood where they are used on additional peak hour services from St Pancras. This in turn has led to a corresponding number of Class 310 units returning to Bletchley from East Ham depot to take their place.

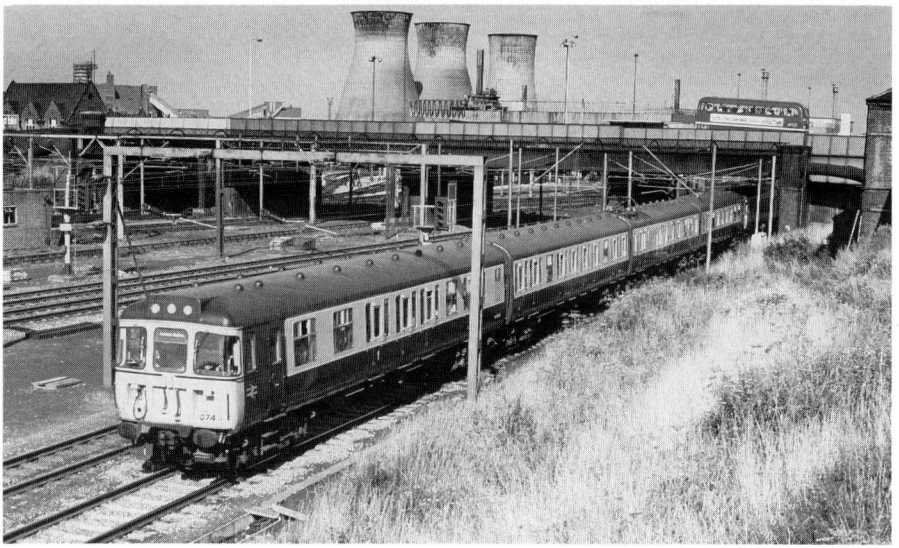

Above:
Displaced or, in BR parlance, cascaded from the Euston services, Class 310 units Nos 310080 and 310082 cross at Fambridge whilst working Wickford to Southminster services on 10 May 1989. The branch line is now reduced to a single track throughout and this is the only crossing place. Both units are in Network SouthEast livery and both have modified windscreens. *Alec Swain*

Right:
The declassification of the former DTC vehicles of Class 310 units allocated to the Provincial Sector has led to sub-class 310/2 being formed as they are refurbished. Here the second unit to be so treated, No 310102, arrives at Witton with a Walsall to Wolverhampton local service on 24 June 1989, bearing the Sector's livery. *Alec Swain*

Below right:
As the previous photograph shows, the light blue and grey colours below window level tend to merge and the third refurbished unit, No 310103, here seen approaching Lea Hall station on a Birmingham New Street to Coventry service on 24 June 1989, shows a much improved version. *Alec Swain*

11 Cravens, Sheffield, ScR Glasgow Suburban Services, Class 311

Introduced: 1967
Purpose: Glasgow to Wemyss Bay/Gourock services
No of cars per unit: Three
Original unit numbers: 092-110
Present unit numbers: 311092-311110 (with gaps)
Equipment manufacturer: AEI (Metrovick)
Traction motor type: MV 222hp (four per unit)
Available horsepower: 888hp (660kW)
Maximum speed: 75mph (120km/hr)
Weight of unit: 129.20 tonnes
Length of unit: 58.36m (191ft 5½in)

Details of Class 311: Built Cravens, Sheffield 1967				
DTS	19.50×2.82m	34.4t	83S	
MBS	19.36×2.82m	56.4t	70S	all Gresley bogies
BDTS	19.50×2.82m	38.4t	83S	

Sets numbered 311092-311110 with gaps

DTS	numbered	76403-76421
MBS	numbered	62163-62181*
BDTS	numbered	76422-76440

* MBS have four AEI 165kW motors

Note that reformations and withdrawals have disturbed the numerical allocation of vehicles to units.

Authorised in 1964, the electrification of the routes from Glasgow to Gourock and Wemyss Bay required a further 19 three-car units and since, by now, the Class 303 trains had settled down, the design was repeated but the trains were to be built this time by Cravens of Sheffield. Delivered in the BR corporate blue livery, rather than the near-Caledonian blue, they must have been quite a disappointment visually, but they have subsequently passed through the same colour changes as the older Class 303 units.

Having been built after the design problems of their earlier brethren had been sorted out, the Class 311 units have led an uneventful life, although all will be progressively withdrawn together with the ScR's remaining unrefurbished examples of Class 303 upon the introduction of new Class 320 units in 1990.

Below:
The MBS vehicle of a Class 311 unit, identical to that of Class 303 except that the area adjoining the guard's and luggage compartment is designated a non-smoking area. *BR*

Bottom:
The first Class 311 unit, No 092, in BR blue livery and retaining the original windscreens, leaves Glasgow Central on a Cathcart circle service on 20 April 1976. *Barry J. Nicolle*

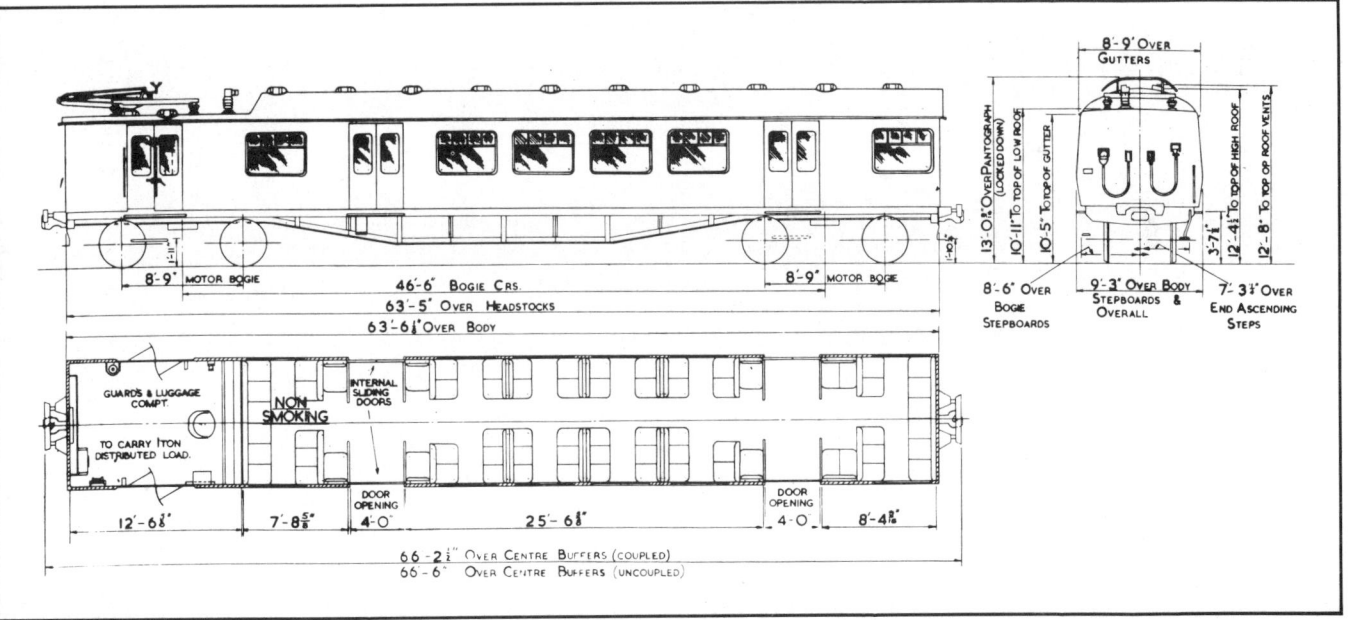

Dalmuir
via Glasgow Central and Singer
311 110
Way out

CR 419

Above left:

Class 311 unit No 311110, in blue/grey livery with 'Strathclyde Transport' logos at Newton on the 16.22 Dalmuir-Lanark service on 4 July 1986. White dots have appeared in the former route indicator and an additional destination indicator has been provided below the original in the roof, giving a comprehensive display, 'Dalmuir – via Glasgow Central and Singer'. *Murdoch Currie*

Above:

Now in Strathclyde PTE orange and black livery, Class 311 unit No 311098 at Milngavie with the 15.20 to Springburn on 11 July 1987. *Murdoch Currie*

Left:

Class 311 unit No 311109, with modified windscreens, arrives at Glasgow Central from Hamilton on 5 August 1979 and passes a previous generation of Glasgow suburban motive power, namely Caledonian Railway 0-4-4T No 419 which was taking part in the station's Centenary exhibition. *Colin Boocock*

Introduced: 1975
Purpose: LMR Birmingham suburban services
ER King's Cross/Liverpool Street outer suburban services
No of cars per unit: Four
Original unit numbers:
312001-312026 (312/0)
312101-312119 (312/1)
312201-312204 (312/2)
Present unit numbers:
312701-312730 (312/0)
312781-312799 (312/1)
Equipment manufacturer: English Electric
Traction motor type: EE 546A (four per unit)
Available horsepower: 1,080hp (806kW)
Maximum speed: 90mph (145km/hr)
Weight of unit: *312/0* 154.5 tonnes
 312/1 154.0 tonnes
Length of unit: 80.975m (265ft 8in)

Details of Class 312: Built York 1976-78

BDTS	19.86×2.82m	34.9t		84S	BT8 bogies
MBS	19.93×2.82m	56.0t		68S	BP14 bogies
TS	19.93×2.82m	30.5t		98S	BT8 bogies
DTC	19.86×2.82m	33.0t	25F	47S	BT8 bogies

Sets numbered 312701-312730 (Class 312/0)
312781-312799 (Class 312/1)

BDTS	numbered	76949-76974	}	312/0
		76994-76997		
		76975-76993		312/1
MBS	numbered	62484-62509*	}	312/1
		62657-62660*		
		62510-62528*		312/1
TS	numbered	71168-71193	}	312/0
		71277-71280		
		71194-71212		312/1
DTC	numbered	78000-78025	}	312/0
		78045-78048		
		78026-78044		312/1

* MBS vehicles have four EE 546 201.5kW motors

Further builds based on successful Class 310 units were introduced in 1975, with four units allocated to the Birmingham area — principally for services to Birmingham International, which serves the airport and Exhibition Centre. Although designed for 90mph running, they had to be restricted to 75mph to enable them to work in multiple with the earlier Class 310 units which were limited to that figure, and a sub-class 312/2 was created for them. The need for this ceased when they joined their 1977 counterparts on the ER, and the four units became Nos 312727-312730, and were classified 312/0.

The original 26 units of Class 312/0, Nos 312001-312026, were built for the King's

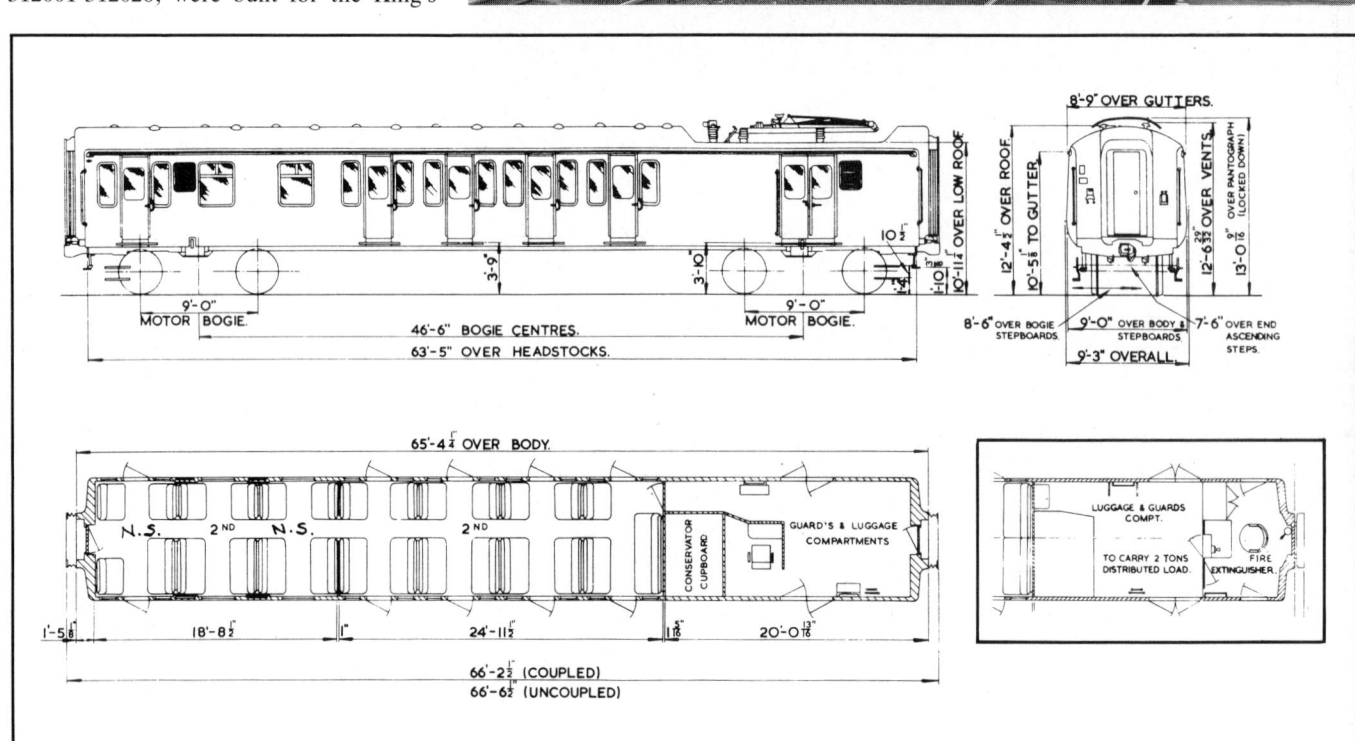

Cross outer suburban services to Royston, but their unsuitability for driver-only operation led to their transfer to Clacton depot for GE lines services once Class 317/1 and 317/2 units had been delivered to Hornsey depot. These sets are now numbered 312701-312726.

The units actually built for the Liverpool Street routes in 1975/76 were required to have dual voltage (6.25/25kV) capability and are classified 312/1 but are otherwise identical and indeed the entire class is now concentrated on GE services and is based at Clacton depot. Originally numbered 312101-312119 they are now Nos 312781-312799.

By now lessons had been learned about wrap-around windscreens and all the Class 312 units were built with the smaller flat type which, until Class 310 was similarly equipped, provided an immediate identification feature.

It is possible that the spread of driver-only operation could lead to the need to find other spheres of operation for these units, and their Class 310 predecessors for that matter, although it is likely that there will always be a certain amount of main line semi-fast work for them, such as Liverpool Street to Ipswich and Harwich Town services.

Above left:
Class 312/1 unit No 312112 in blue livery and with unpainted window surrounds passes Stratford bound for Liverpool Street on 12 September 1979. Its new unit number, 792, is also displayed on the centre windscreen. *Peter Kynaston*

Below left:
The MBS vehicle of a Class 312 unit, again very similar to that of Class 310 except that to provide a gangway for passenger access throughout, the guard's and luggage compartment has been rearranged, there being no longer a separate single door for the guard's use; instead one of the double doors now opens inwards for his use. The inset shows the Class 310 arrangement before refurbishment. *BR*

Above right:
The restyled front end of Class 312/0 unit No 312003 (now 312703), which makes an interesting comparison with that of Class 310. Gone are the wrap-around windscreens, and the jumper cable sockets, together with the brake pipe and main reservoir pipe isolating cocks, are now fully exposed. The black window surrounds certainly improve matters. *BR*

Right:
Class 312 unit No 312204 (now No 312730), one of the four originally allocated to the Birmingham area, was painted in the West Midlands PTE colours of yellow and blue 'to assess public reaction to a new livery'. At least it enabled the much-criticised yellow end to be extended the full length of the vehicle! *BR*

Left:
Class 312/1 unit No 312788 departs from Ipswich on 18 May 1985 with the 14.20 to Liverpool Street, this being the first Saturday of scheduled electric working to Ipswich. Note that an automotive-type headlight is fitted in the aperture below the driver's windscreen. *David Brown*

Below:
In Network SouthEast livery, Class 312/2 unit No 312784 enters Southend Victoria heading a service from Liverpool Street on 10 May 1989, the rear unit still being in blue/grey livery. *Alec Swain*

Right:
MBS vehicle No 62513 of Class 312/2 unit No 312784, showing the altered door arrangements when compared with the following photograph. *Alec Swain*

Below right:
MBSO vehicle No M62071 of the first Class 310/0 unit No 046 showing the additional inwards-opening door for the use of the guard. *BR*

62513

M 62071
Guard
MBSO

The Second Generation BR Designs

The evolution of the Class 313 units, based on the 1972 Class 445 prototypes, has been fully described in Part 10 of this series, and it is perhaps sufficient to remind readers of their essential features when compared with the classes that had preceded them. The slam door was at last banished — the application of sliding doors to the ScR's Class 303 and 311 trains had really been ahead of its time so far as the engineering factions were concerned. Looking back it now seems incredible that slam-door stock was still being built in 1978, represented by the last of the Class 312 units, when surely the long-term planners already had driver-only operation in mind. No doubt it was a question of development time, and with the 1965 Class 310 design being readily available it was a simple matter to order further examples. Nevertheless, the principles of integral construction had been accepted for these EMUs, and for locomotive-hauled stock, so one still wonders why the Class 445 high-density design was not adapted for an outer-suburban role as well.

A business requirement stipulated that coupling and uncoupling should be fully automatic, under the control of the driver, and that a shunter would not be required to attend to air hoses and jumper cables. Therefore the Tightlock automatic coupling, incorporating the necessary pneumatic and electrical connections, became the standard for all future EMU classes and enabled the front end design to be tidied up. This had the disadvantage of precluding multiple working with earlier EMU types, and necessitated the provision of adaptor couplings for emergency use should it be necessary to couple to a conventional drawhook; however, these disadvantages were outweighed by the simplicity and ease of operation. The braking system too had to change, to the Westcode type, which required only three

train wires running the full length of the unit to provide the necessary switching for the electropneumatic braking steps. Thus, so far as EMU trains were concerned, the air brake pipe hose and all its attendant risks of leakages and bursts passed into history.

There also appeared a new type of bogie, the BX1 and later variants, which incorporated air suspension and this too has remained the standard, giving passengers a superb ride under all conditions of loading as the system allows for the air pressure within the rubber suspension units to be adjusted as the vehicle loses or gains passengers.

Following the difficulties with the passenger-operated doors on the Class 313 units, as chronicled in Part 10, the Class 314 trains reverted to the traditional 'traincrew open and close' system, which leads to a great deal of heat loss when doors are opened unnecessarily at off-peak times, or when trains are standing at terminal stations. However, the 'passenger open' facility, under overall control of the traincrew, returned with the Class 315, and indeed this and subsequent builds have even incorporated a 'passenger close' feature to enable an individual to close the doors behind him once he has entered the train.

There was also a major change in the configuration of the traction motors, in that rather than concentrate them on a motor vehicle in the middle of the unit formation, they were applied to the outer vehicles. This meant that four large (and heavy) motors could be replaced by eight smaller and lighter ones which in turn gave the potential for rheostatic braking.

This feature, sometimes known as dynamic braking, uses the natural tendency of a motor to act as a generator to provide a retardation effect when braking is required, and the conventional disc

brakes are not normally applied until speed has fallen to around 15mph, when the rheostatic braking effort becomes insufficient to finally bring the train to a stand within the required stopping distance. The savings on brake discs and pads are considerable as their lives are extended, although the adjustment of the electrical equipment to provide the necessary safeguards should rheostatic braking not be established has, in the past, proved troublesome.

Finally, this design saw the end of the traditional guard's/luggage compartment, and the guard now operated from an unoccupied driving compartment wherein were sited the necessary door controls. Not surprisingly, the intrusion of the guard into the hitherto hallowed domain of the driver resulted in some rumblings in trade union circles, but it did enable most of the floorspace to be given over to the carriage of passengers. The lack of a luggage area was hardly noticed in the inner suburban areas where these trains were to work, and the vestibule area which gave access to the driving compartment was in any case still for the exclusive use of the traincrew.

Thus this design of train, which dates back to 1972, continues to serve BR very well indeed in both ac overhead line and dc third rail form, but it was intended for high-density and inner suburban services. Thus something a little more sophisticated was required for longer distances and the experience gained with the construction of Mk 3 locomotive-hauled stock was sufficient for the go-ahead to be given for the planning of the next generation.

Below:
Class 315 EMU No 315816 on Bethnal Green bank with the 13.19 Liverpool Street-Cheshunt on 22 November 1986.
Brian Morrison

Introduced: 1979
Purpose: Glasgow Central Low Level (Argyle Line) services
No of cars per unit: Three
Original unit numbers: 314201-314216
Equipment manufacturer: Brush/GEC
Traction motor type: 314201-314206 Brush TM61-53, 314207-314216 GEC G310AZ, eight per unit
Available horsepower: 880hp (657kW)
Maximum speed: 75mph (120km/hr)
Weight of unit: 102 tonnes
Length of unit: 60.808m (199ft 6in)

In 1970 a survey of the former Caledonian Railway Glasgow Central Low Level line (closed in 1964) was undertaken with a view to it being incorporated into the existing system to provide a much-needed connection between the North and South Clyde systems. However, it was not until 1974 that approval, and a 75% grant, was given to enable planning to commence, and major construction work actually began in July 1976. Sixteen three-car units were required for the new services and delivery of Class 314 trains, to the same external general design as the Class 313 units (see *BR Fleet Survey 10*, Section 21), enabled public services to be introduced early in November 1979 and the through journeys that became possible, such as

Below:
The drawing shows the TS vehicle of a Class 314 unit, based on that of Class 313 but with reduced seating, and therefore a greater standing area, around the double leaf sliding doors. Note that the vertical door handles are shown, a feature fully described in *BR Fleet Survey 10* under Class 313 but never in fact fitted to Class 314. *BR*

Bottom:
Class 314 EMU No 314213 awaits delivery in the yard at BREL York on 12 July 1979. Note the match vehicle No B734425 attached to the Tightlock coupler which enabled the unit to be locomotive-hauled. One was provided at each end of the formation. *Alec Swain*

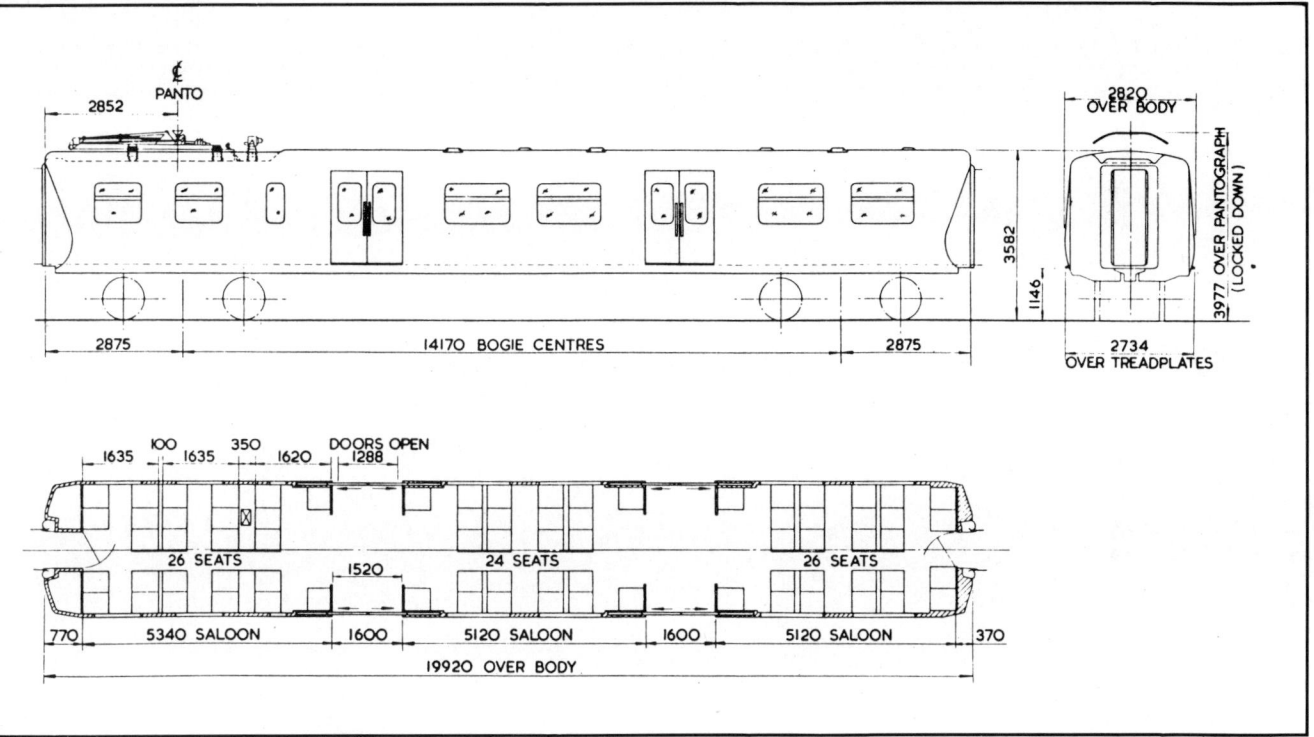

Dumbarton to Motherwell, did much to take pressure off other Glasgow transport services.

With Westcode type electro pneumatic braking and Tightlock auto couplers the new trains could not work in multiple with the earlier Class 303 and 311 units but allocation to dedicated services has meant that this has not been too much of a problem. The seating layout differs from that of the Class 313, in that although the standard 3+2 seating is provided in the centre of each seating bay, only single seats are located adjacent to the vestibules by the double-leaf power doors in order to maximise the standing area available in the peak hours. Thus, with no luggage area as such, each DMS-TS-DMS formation can seat 212 passengers, this being 20 less than their GN counterparts.

Electrically the Class 314 units have the benefit of thyristor control and, with no requirement for a 6.25/25kV capability, have proved to be most successful in service.

Details of Class 314: Built York 1979

DMS	19.80×2.82m	34.5t 68S	all BX1 bodies
TS	19.92×2.82m	33.0t 76S	all BX1 bodies
DMS	19.80×2.82m	34.5t 68S	all BX1 bodies

Sets numbered 314201-314216

DMS numbered 64583-64594*
64595-64614†
TS 71450-71465‡

* Has four Brush TM61-53 82.125kW motors
† Has four GEC G310AZ 82.125kW motors
‡ Carries the pantograph

Below:
Here Class 314 unit No 314210 enters Motherwell with the 10.48 from Dalmuir on 10 September 1981, showing how the black window surrounds and end door in fact break up the yellow end, and produce quite an acceptable effect. This particular unit has evidently come into contact with conventional buffers as the crumpled footholds beneath the frontal lighting testify! Both destination indicators are put to good use by the ScR, and the display here (already set for the return journey) says 'Dalmuir via Blantyre, Glasgow Central and Singer'.
Les Bertram

Right:
All Class 314 units have now been repainted into Strathclyde PTE orange and black livery, this example being No 314204 at Helensburgh Central with the 11.54 service to Airdrie on 25 May 1987. Here the destination indicators show 'Airdrie via Glasgow Queen St – Limited Stop'. *Murdoch Currie*

Below right:
The destination displays 'Special' so it comes as no surprise that Class 314 unit No 314212 is working a 15.00 special service from the somewhat damp platforms of Motherwell to Coatbridge Central on 12 August 1987.
Murdoch Currie

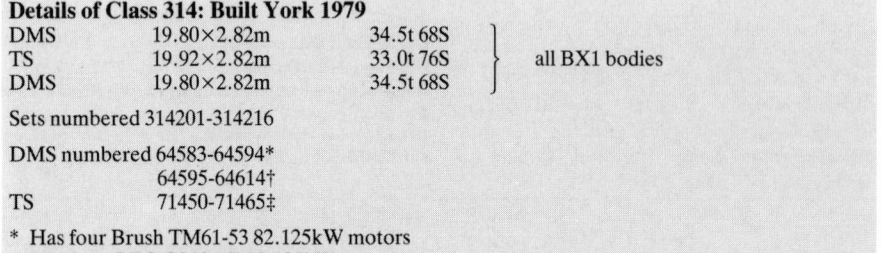

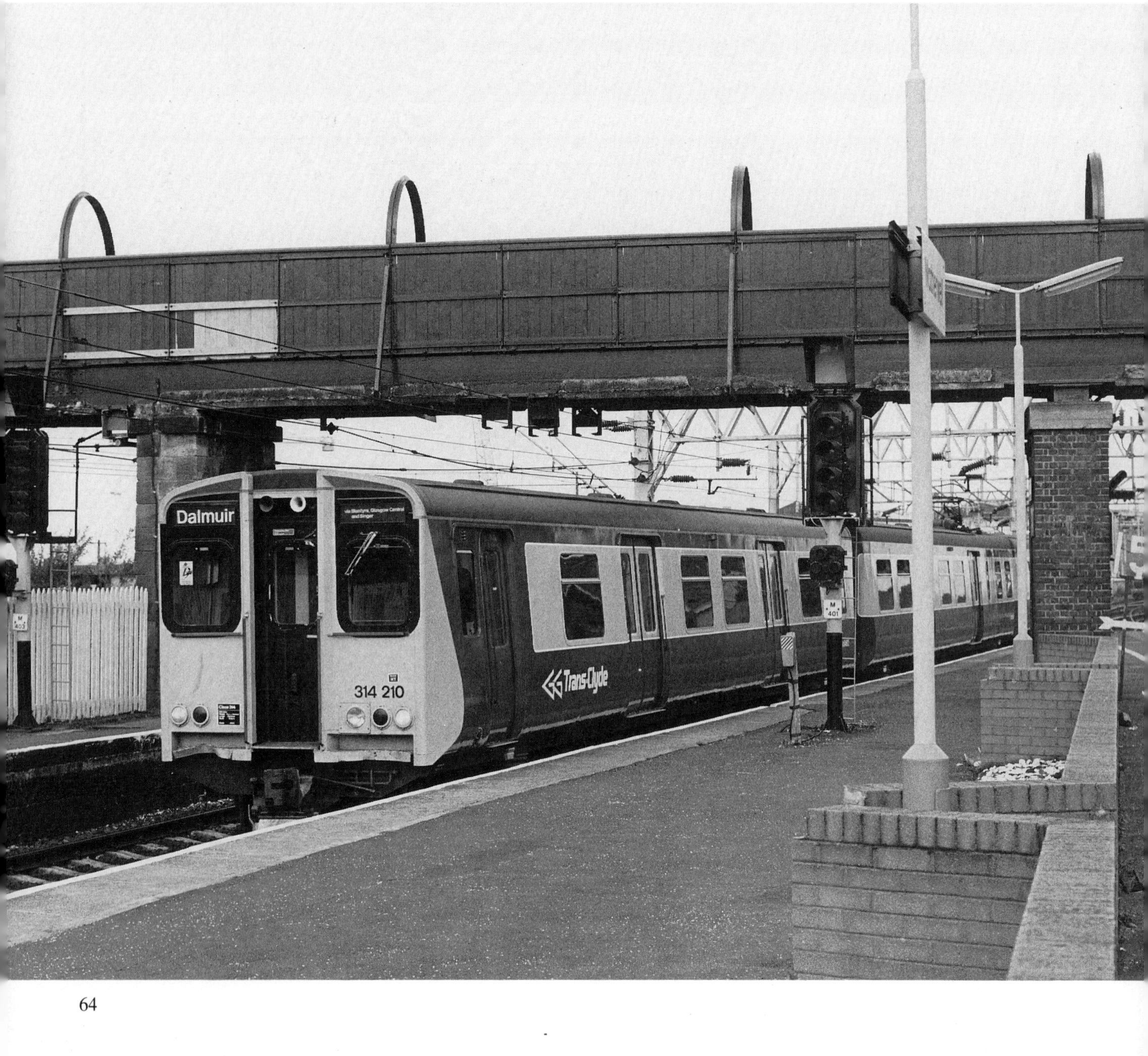

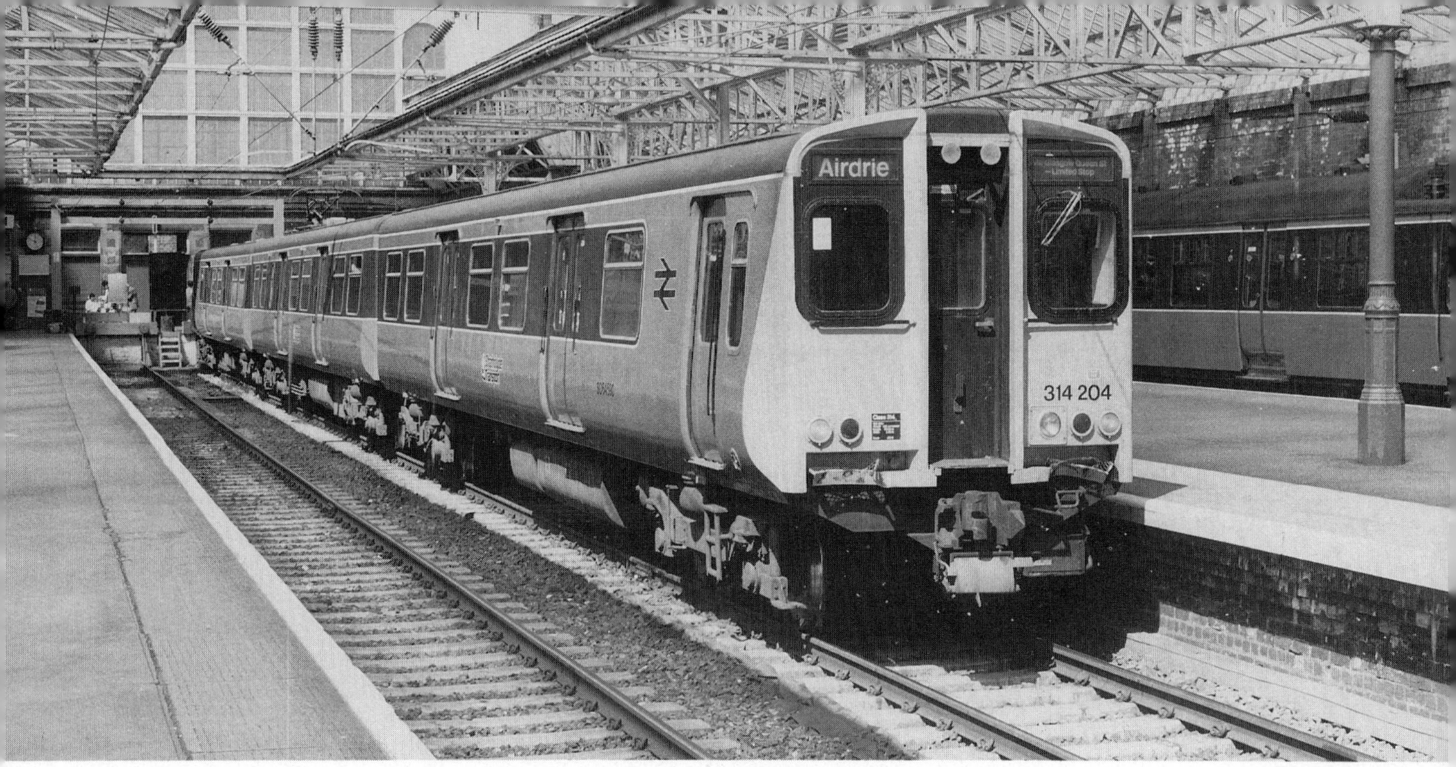
Airdrie
314 204

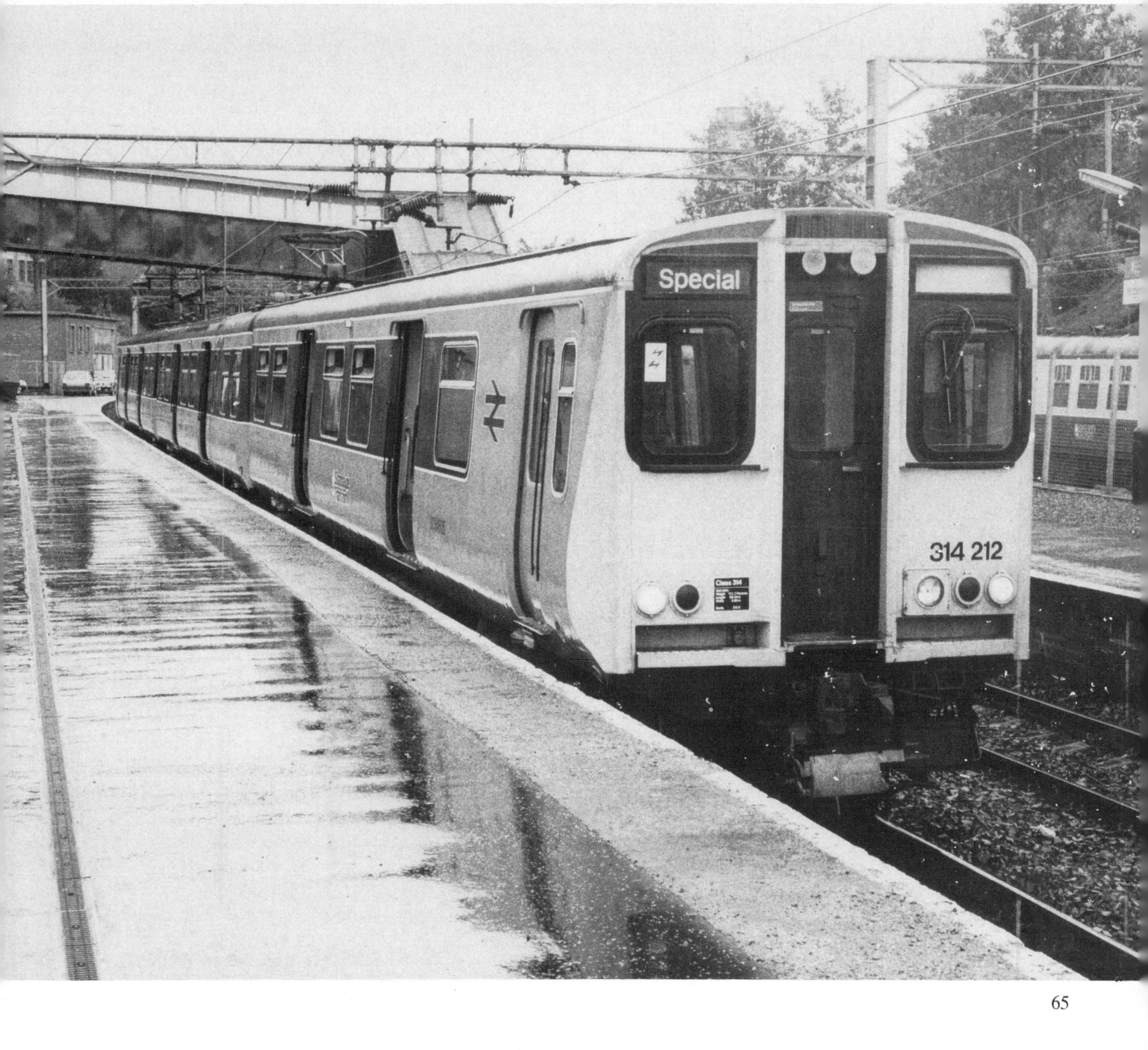
Special
314 212

Introduced: 1980
Purpose: Liverpool Street to Shenfield services
No of cars per unit: Four
Original unit numbers: 315801-315861
Equipment manufacturer: Brush/GEC
Traction motor type: 315801-315841 Brush TM61-53, 315842-315861 GEC G310AZ, eight per unit
Available horsepower: 880hp (657kW)
Maximum speed: 75mph (120km/hr)
Weight of unit: 127.8 tonnes
Length of unit: 81.0m (265ft 9in)

When the need arose to replace the LNER-designed Class 306 trains, all that was necessary was to continue the Class 314 build but with the addition of another vehicle to make a four-car unit — such were the benefits of having an established and proven design. The 61 units were in fact ordered in 1976, with

Above right:
The first Class 315 unit, No 315801, leaves Shenfield station during commissioning trials from Ilford depot on 16 December 1980. The four-character route indicator was in use at the time, displaying the code 5B69 for this empty stock working. *BR*

Below:
This drawing shows the DMS vehicle of a Class 315 unit, when the seating layout around the double-leaf doors reverted to that of the Class 313. Note the half-width driving compartment and the end vestibule area, which is not available for passenger use when it is required by the driver or guard and the sliding door giving access to the passenger saloon is locked. This 'waste' of floor space, and the 'pocket' into which the single-leaf sliding door moves when it is opened, have taxed the ingenuity of vehicle designers for some years and, as we shall see, has only comparatively recently been solved to the satisfaction of all concerned. *BR*

the now-standard thyristor control and 6.25/25kV capability; however, such was the rate of conversion of the GE lines that it proved possible to amend the specification in 1978 to provide for 25kV operation only, thus removing a potential source of trouble. The Class 315 units, formed DMS-TS-TS-DMS, were eventually built during 1980/81 and, with an internal layout more akin to that of the Class 313, provided 318 seats compared with 168 of the three-car Class 306. To be fair, however, the latter operated as nine-car trains in the peak (504 seats) whereas the Class 315 units run as eight-car formations (636 seats). Nevertheless, their coming was certainly to the benefit of the GE commuter.

The continued programme of conversion to 25kV-only operation enabled the Class 315 units to work the Chingford and Enfield services as well from January 1984, and they continue to give excellent service

carrying Network SouthEast livery in place of their original blue/grey, and may be seen at locations as far afield as Hertford East and Southend Victoria. It is on these longer-distance services that their lack of toilet accommodation is something of a disadvantage, particularly when vandalism has forced the closure of many on-station facilities.

One minor alteration concerns the single-leaf doors, which are no longer available for public use even when they are located intermediately in an eight-car train, and the passenger control buttons have been blanked off. This means that the adjacent vestibules are no longer available to standing passengers as the internal manually operated sliding doors are now kept locked, with their emergency handles removed and blanked off. To provide a means of escape in an emergency, handles have been provided above the double-leaf doors to enable passengers to release the

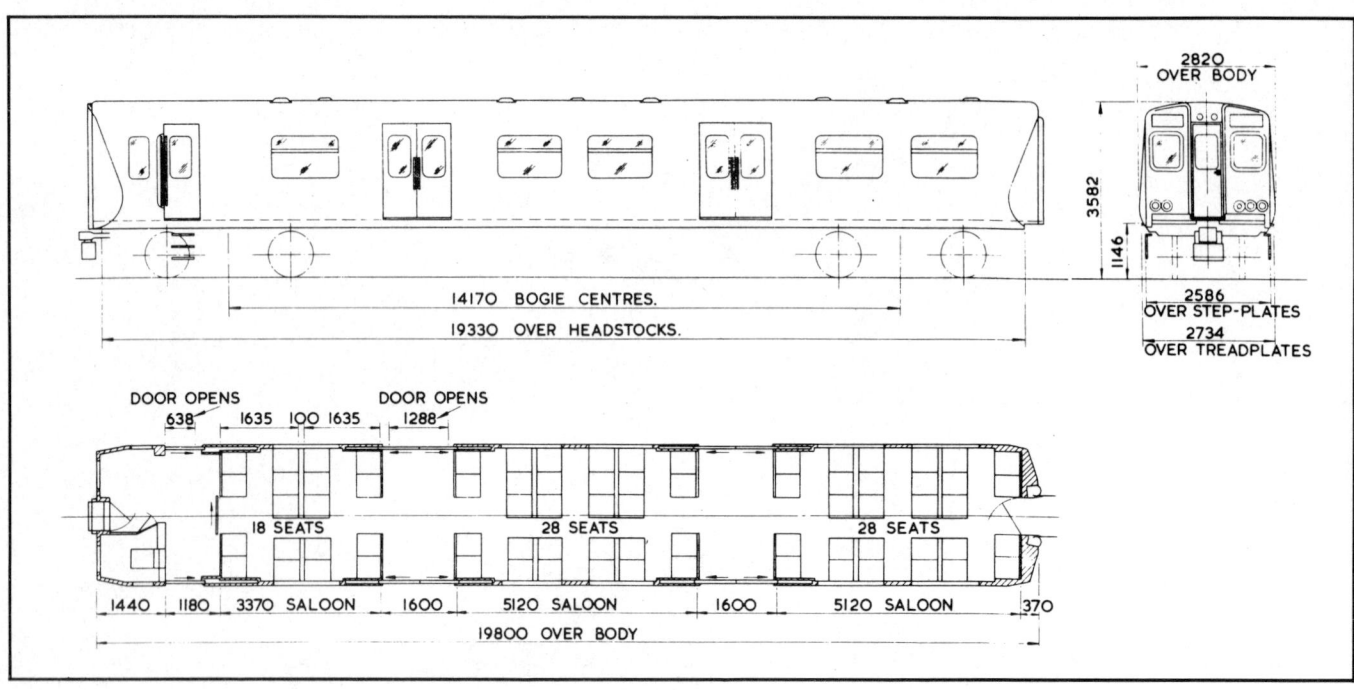

door-operating air pressure, and thus open them to allow the passengers to alight onto the trackside.

The destination indicator above the right-hand side window is no longer in use and perhaps the GE lines could put this to good use, as the ScR has done, to show the route to be taken. The writer has observed the new Class 321 units displaying 'Cambridge via Tottenham Hale', so how about 'Hertford East via Seven Sisters' for the Class 315 units?

Details of Class 315: Built York 1980/81

DMS	19.80×2.82m	35.2t	74S	
TS	19.92×2.82m	25.5t	86S	all BX1 bogies
TS	19.92×2.82m	31.9t	84S	
DMS	19.80×2.82m	35.2t	74S	

Sets numbered 315801-315861

DMS numbered 64461-64542*
64543-64582†

TS numbered 71281-71341

TS numbered 71389-71449‡

* Has four Brush TH61-53 82.125kW motors
† Has four GEC G310AZ 82.135kW motors
‡ Carries the pantograph

Below:
On loan to the LMR for preliminary driver training prior to the introduction of the 'Bedpan' services, Class 315 unit No 315807 pauses at Luton on 17 March 1981. A dispute over the manning of the Class 317 units intended for the Midland Suburban Electrification (MSE), as it was officially known, had led to the trade unions declaring them 'black' and they could not be used. *BR*

Bottom:
Beneath the vaulted roof of Liverpool Street station Class 315 unit No 315849 waits to depart with the 10.49 Enfield Town service on 20 October 1984. These units were the first to have passenger-controlled doors, with push buttons either side of the doorway, and the door obstruction/hazard lights at roof level are illuminated in this photograph. The route indicator is no longer in use. *Alex Dasi-Sutton*

Above right:
Repainted into Network SouthEast livery, Class 315 unit No 315850 calls at Seven Kings with a Gidea Park service on 2 July 1988. The route indicator is no longer in use and has been painted over. *Alec Swain*

Right:
To allow driver-only operation on the Romford to Upminster service Class 315 units are now used. Here unit No 315802 awaits departure from Upminster on 27 May 1989 alongside tracks which lead, in the distance, to London Underground Ltd's Upminster depot. There is no rail connection between the two systems. *Alec Swain*

Below:
The first Class 315 unit, No 315801, now in Network SouthEast livery, leaves Broxbourne with an afternoon Hertford East to Liverpool Street service on 17 June 1989. *Alec Swain*

The Third Generation BR Designs

At the same time as the Class 315 units were being built at York, visitors could see the development work on the bodysides of what were to be the Class 317 trains, destined for the Midland Suburban Electrification (MSE), and later to be dubbed the 'Bedpan' units after the Bedford to St Pancras route on which they worked. Based on the Mk 3 locomotive-hauled integral coach, but reduced in length to take account of the routes over which they were to work, tests proved that the shell would support the underframe equipment of the motor coach in particular and the design was soon approved.

I have chosen to regard these as the Third Generation for two reasons; firstly, the change to the Mk 3 body profile and secondly, a major policy change which caused the traction motor configuration to revert to the original concept of four large motors concentrated in one vehicle! Having previously extolled the virtues of having eight smaller motors one is now faced with having to explain why this arrangement was suddenly regarded, by the designers, as unsatisfactory. The decision was no doubt based on costs, due to both the initial need to purchase twice the number of motors and the subsequent cost of their maintenance. It was also thought undesirable, in certain quarters, to have high voltage dc jumper cables running from the pantograph coach to the outer vehicles.

To accommodate inter-unit gangway connections, now considered necessary to enable peak hour passengers to make their way to less crowded parts of the train, the front end design had to be changed – not for the better as it turned out. In fact the design originally produced for the Class 210 DEMU was used (see *BR Fleet Survey 9*), with a rather ugly centre 'box' above the gangway which was cut away either side to accommodate the warning horns. As we will see later the repositioning of the warning horns enabled the roof profile to be tidied up on later versions.

Below:
A contrast in front end designs between second and third generation EMUs, although despite the differences in appearance, the couplings are compatible. Class 315 No 315843 forming the 13.47 to Chingford alongside Class 321 No 321310 at Liverpool Street on 17 February 1989. *Alex Dasi-Sutton*

15 BREL Derby/York, LMR and ER London Suburban Services, Class 317

Introduced: 1981 (317/1), 1985 (317/2)
Purpose: St Pancras/Moorgate to Bedford services (317/1)
King's Cross to Royston services (317/2)
No of cars per unit: Four
Original unit numbers:
317301-317348 (317/0)
317349-317372 (317/2)
Equipment manufacturer: GEC
Traction motor type: G315BZ
Available horsepower: 1,328hp (996kW)
Maximum speed: 100mph (160km/hr)
Weight of unit: 137.35 tonnes
Length of unit: 80.72m (264ft 10in)

The plan to electrify from St Pancras to Bedford, together with the branch to Moorgate, was approved in late November 1976 and in the following years much was done to improve track alignment, raise bridges and resignal in preparation. The actual erection of the overhead catenary was well advanced by the summer of 1979, working south from Bedford where the construction trains were based, and the overhead line was energised from Bedford to just south of Luton on 12 January 1981

to enable driver training to commence. The Midland commuters, who had endured the Class 127 Rolls-Royce-engined DMUs for many years, must have sighed with relief at the sight of all this progress but little did they know at the time just how long they would have to wait to travel in their first electric train!

No less than 48 four-car units were required, as the frequency was to be increased and services were to run through to Moorgate throughout the day rather than just in the peak hours as before. In deference to railmen working in the tunnel sections, and acknowledging modern standards of hygiene, the TC vehicles were fitted with two controlled emission toilets from which the effluent was directed into an underslung tank, to be emptied at intervals by special equipment at the new Cricklewood depot. The availability of staff at Derby Litchurch Lane, together with their experience of building the Mk 3 sleeping coaches, which were similarly equipped, resulted in these vehicles being built there. They were then hauled to York to join the other three vehicles and be

formed into units. Thus the toilet facilities were now available for use whilst the train was standing at a station and the time-honoured instructions were no longer displayed! The specification called for limited first class accommodation, just 22 seats, but no sooner had the first units been built than a decision was made to declassify it and staff were sent down specially from Derby to remove the first class seating and fit standard class in its place. As later events will show, this declassification was not to be permanent!

The problem was that the Class 317s were designed from the outset for driver-only operation, with the driver being in control of the doors, and the trade unions

Below:
These drawings of the DTS(B) vehicles of (A) Class 317/1 and (B) Class 317/2 units show the different configurations of the invalid/luggage areas which can be made available in off-peak hours by locking the internal sliding door. The circuitry is so arranged that the adjacent double-leaf doors do not then respond to the passenger control buttons, thus giving a secure area for the carriage of mails etc. *BR*

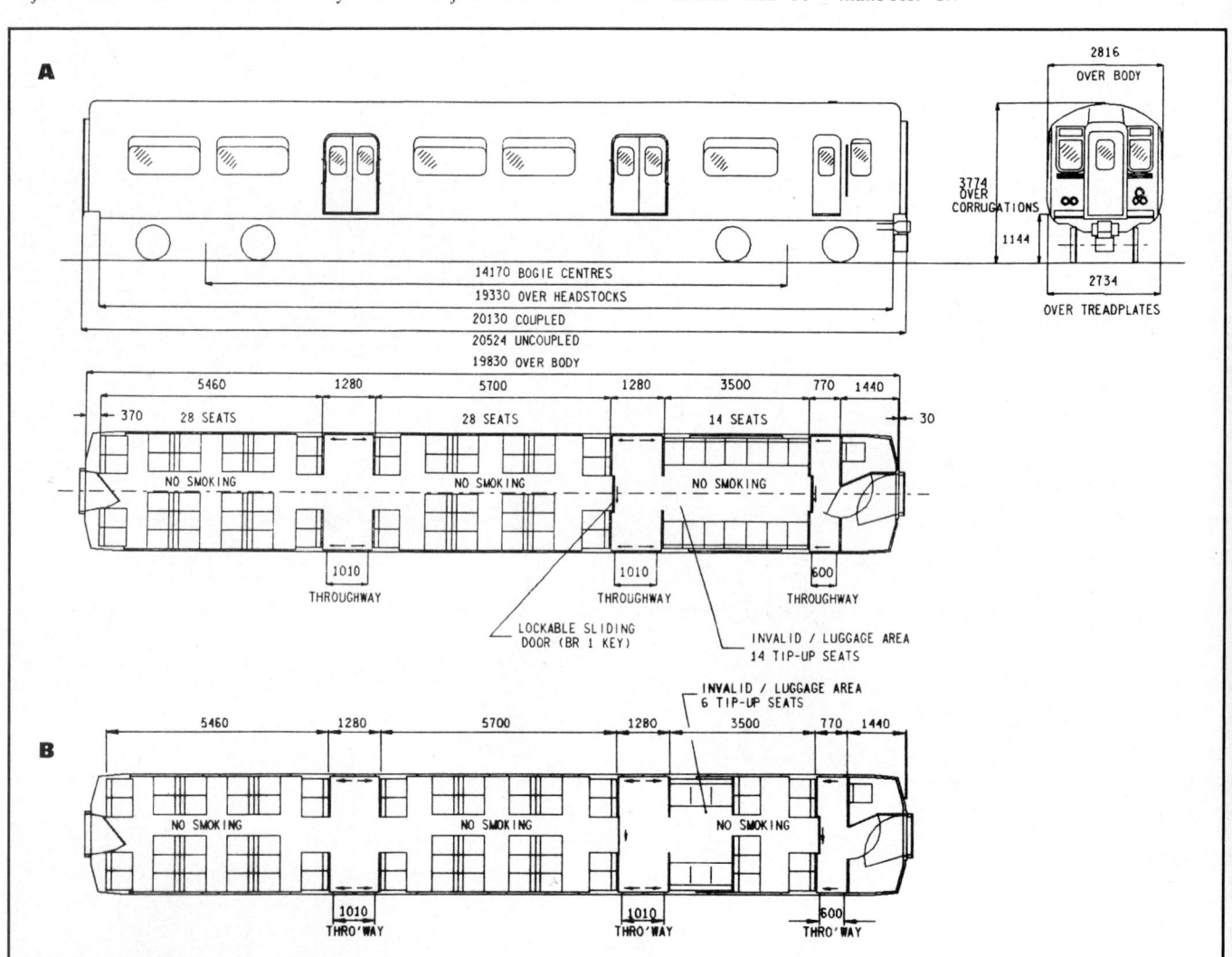

were violently opposed to this principle, which was to be its first application on BR. Nevertheless the work continued and, perhaps unwisely, it was announced that electric trains would start to run from Bedford to Moorgate on 17 May 1982, despite the fact that the unions had not yet agreed to the driver-only principle. The new trains were declared 'black', and no driver training on them took place.

A bitter dispute arose, culminating in a series of national strikes, but eventually an agreement was reached and the first public services of any consequence commenced from 18 April 1983, with just four trains each way operating between Bedford and St Pancras. Some preliminary driver training had taken place, particularly at Bedford, using a Class 315 unit on loan from Ilford depot and carrying a guard, naturally! This seemed a little unusual at the time, but at least it gave the drivers some experience of electric traction – not just the trains but also the overhead line equipment which is itself subject to quite complicated instructions and was quite foreign to the Midland men. It meant, however, that some of the early Class 317 units had been stored for almost two years without turning a wheel in service; in fact, the first unit, No 317301, had been extensively damaged in a shunting mishap at the new Cricklewood depot and a replacement DTS vehicle had to be built. This incident is still reflected in the unit formations today, where unit No 301 now contains DTS vehicle No 77024 and the replacement, the 'new' No 77000, is formed in unit No 325! This unforeseen period of storage at least gave the opportunity to declassify the TC vehicle and undertake some of the preparatory work.

Meanwhile, of course, the Class 127 DMU trains had to soldier on, and many commuters found alternative ways to travel, such was the poor standard of service offered, with frequent cancellations, late running and failures in service. It was not until 11 July 1983 that the full electric service, including that to Moorgate, commenced but even then the backlog of driver training meant that some peak hour workings to and from St Pancras were still in the hands of DMU trains. Even then the problems were not over, since transformer mountings were found to be suspect and modifications were necessary. So serious was the problem that for a time maintenance staff were positioned at strategic locations, such as Luton, to check the security of the underframe-mounted transformers as units passed through. However, all problems were eventually overcome and the service on offer soon enticed back those commuters who had deserted the railway, as evidenced by the full car parks at Bedford and intermediate stations.

To replace the Great Northern outer suburban Class 312 slam-door stock, with driver-only operation in mind, a further 24 units were ordered from York incorporating the improved front end design mentioned earlier and with convection heating rather than pressure ventilation for the passenger saloons. Thus sub-class 317/2 was created.

Meanwhile the then-Greater London Council (GLC) had initiated a joint study of cross-London rail routes which was completed in October 1984 and this was to have a profound effect on the future of the Class 317 units, since it involved the reopening of the Snow Hill connection between Holborn Viaduct and Farringdon, thus linking the 750V dc third rail SR network and the 25kV ac overhead line LMR Moorgate branch. Further dual voltage trains were therefore required, and these materialised in 1987 as the Class 319 units which I have dealt with in *BR Fleet Survey 10*, leaving the Class 317 units to find new homes, or to be 'cascaded' to the Euston and King's Cross outer suburban services, to quote BR parlance. This, of course, required the first class accommodation, removed before they had entered service, to be reinstated. In addition, the underslung toilet tanks were removed, and these modifications created a sub-class 317/1 for a while as initial transfers to the ER took place.

The Thameslink service has proved highly successful and, pending the building of more Class 319 units, some of the original 'Bedpan' Class 317s have returned to work peak hour services from St Pancras.

Details of Class 317/1: Built 1981-82; Class 317/2: Built 1985-87

DTS(A)	19.83×2.82m	29.44t			74S	BT13 bogies
MS	19.92×2.82m	49.76t			79S	BP 20 bogies
TC	19.92×2.82m	28.87t		22F	46S	BT13 bogies
DTS(B)	19.83×2.82m	29.28t			74S	BT13 bogies

Sets	numbered	317301-317348	(317/1)
		317349-317372	(317/2)
DTS	numbered	77000-77095	(317/1)
		77200-77239	(317/2 1985-86 build)
		77280-77287	(317/2 1987 build)
MS	numbered	62661-62708*	(317/1)
		62846-62865*	(317/2 1985-86 build)
		62886-62889*	(317/2 1987 build
TC	numbered	71577-71624	(317/1)
		71734-71753	(317/2 1985-86 build)
		71762-71765	(317/2 1987 build)

*MS has four GEC G315BZ 247.5kW motors and pantograph

Above left:
As a foretaste of the forthcoming Ayrshire electrification scheme, a Railfair was staged at Ayr and Class 317 unit No 317335 made the long journey from London to be on display over the weekend of 29/30 October 1983.
Colin Boocock

Left:
The third rail is already in position for the Thameslink service as Class 317 unit No 317308 enters Farringdon on 16 July 1987 with the 13.58 Luton-Moorgate service, having just negotiated the flyunder beneath the adjacent LUL tracks to the right.
Kevin Lane

Below:
Displaced from the 'Bedpan' line, Class 317/1 unit No 317310 arrives at Northampton at the head of a Birmingham New Street to Euston service on 13 May 1989, with both units sporting Network SouthEast livery.
Alec Swain

Above:
Another exile, Class 317/1 unit No 317336, is formed at the rear of this King's Cross to Royston service on 19 June 1989 passing the one-time goods shed at Ashwell & Morden. The leading unit is still in blue/grey livery. *Alec Swain*

Left:
The first Class 317/2 unit, No 317349, at Hornsey depot on 4 December 1985, showing the efforts that had been made to improve the front end, with the yellow area not being carried quite so far round on to the bodyside. The relocation of the warning horns to a position below the underframe enables the roof profile to be restored and the marker, tail and headlights are now contained within a neat block which is hinged to allow easy access for lamp renewal. The unit number is displayed either side of the gangway connection and the hopper windows are now glazed. *BR*

Below left:
Now in Network SouthEast livery the first Class 317/2 unit, No 317349, calls at Welwyn North with a Royston to King's Cross service on 19 June 1989. The unit number is now displayed on one side only, whilst the NSE 'chevron' occupies the former position of the data panel above the right-hand front lighting block. *Alec Swain*

Introduced: 1986
Purpose: Glasgow to Ardrossan services
No of cars per unit: Three
Original unit numbers: 318250-318270
Equipment manufacturer: GEC
Traction motor type: G315BZ
Available horsepower: 1,328hp (996kW)
Maximum speed: 100mph (160km/hr)
Weight of unit: 107.51 tonnes
Length of unit: 59.58m (195ft 5½in)

In February 1979 Strathclyde Regional Council announced a further electrification scheme for the former Glasgow & South Western Railway lines to Ayr and Ardrossan, adding some 40 route miles to the ScR's electrified network. The entire route was modernised and the attendant rationalisation of trackwork helped to control the cost of the scheme, which had Government financial support. In June 1985 approval was given for a further extension from Ardrossan to Largs, again with financial support from the Government.

With a proven design in production, all that was necessary was to place a further order for Class 317/2 type units but

reduced to a three-car DTS-PMS-DTS formation. The first of the Class 318 units was delivered in June 1986 and, with work progressing well, it proved possible to introduce electric services to Ayr in September of that year, to Ardrossan in November and to Largs in January 1987 – some four months ahead of schedule.

It is perhaps rather ironic that a reduced demand for travel in the inner-city areas caused by a shift in population, released sufficient Class 303 units to enable them to be refurbished to supplement the new Class 318s; nevertheless this must have contributed to the financial viability of the initial scheme.

Above right:
The first Class 318 unit, No 318250 in Strathclyde PTE orange and black livery, poses for publicity purposes. Using the Class 317/2 front end, the slightly reduced yellow area and black edging has given an angular appearance which disguises the traditional 'tumblehome' of the bodysides. Note that only one of the destination indicators is now used and that the unit number is displayed on one side only. *BR*

Below:
The DTS(A) vehicle of a Class 318 unit, with a single toilet compartment and space for a wheelchair. *BR*

Details of Class 318: Built York 1985-87

DTS(A)	19.83×2.82m	30.01t	66S	BT13 bogies
MS	19.92×2.82m	50.90t	79S	BP20 bogies
DTS(B)	19.83×2.82m	29.60t	71S	BT13 bogies
Sets	numbered	318250-318270		
DTS(A)	numbered	77260-77279, 77289		
MS	numbered	62866-62885, 62890*		
DTS(B)	numbered	77240-77259, 77288		

*MS has four GEC G315BZ 247.5kW motors and pantograph

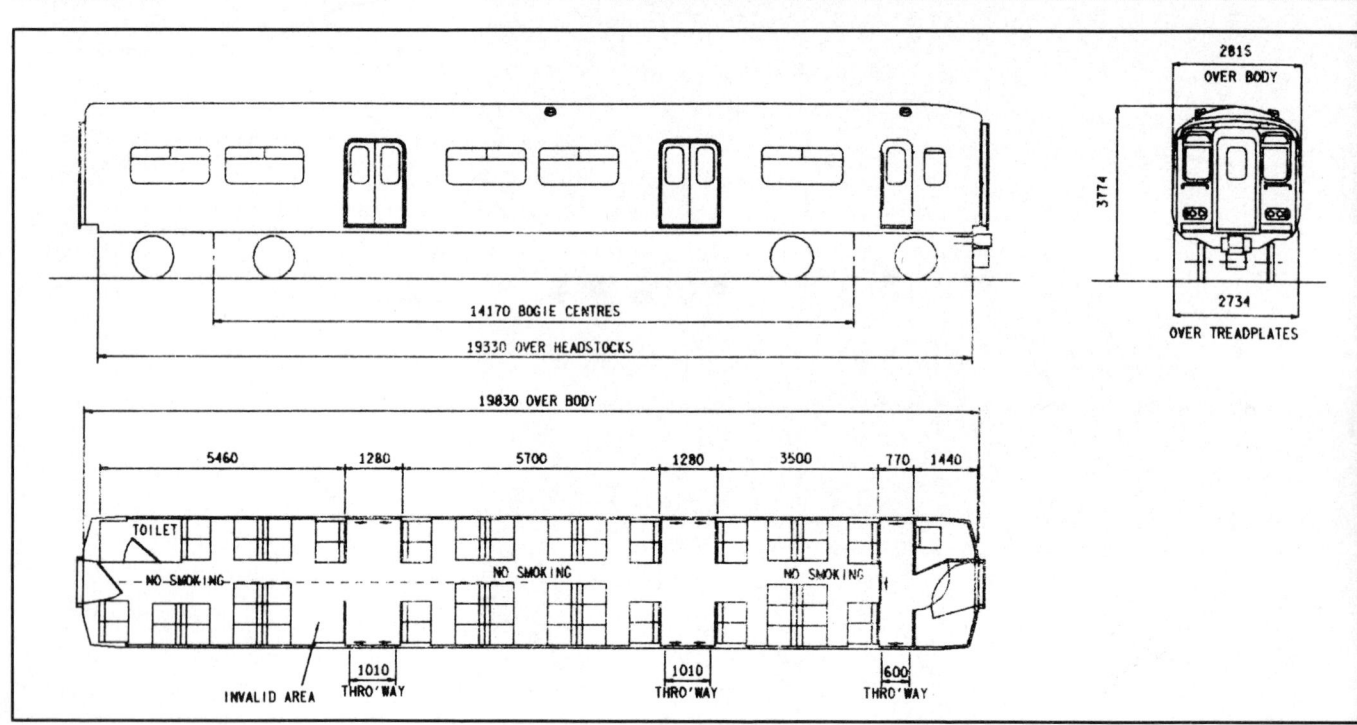

17 BREL York, ER and LMR Outer Suburban Services, Class 321

Introduced: 1988
Purpose: Liverpool Street to Southend/Cambridge services
Euston to Birmingham via Northampton services
No of cars per unit: Four
Original unit numbers: 321301-321371 plus
Equipment manufacturer: Brush
Traction motor type: TM2141B
Available horsepower: 1,438hp (1,072kW)
Maximum speed: 100mph (160km/hr)
Weight of unit: 138.68 tonnes
Length of unit: 80.92m (265ft 5¾in)

It was widely known that the Director of Network SouthEast was not happy with the appearance of multiple-unit trains such as the Class 317/2, even though the front end had been tidied up. Just as in Glasgow back in the late 1950s, it was thought that an eyecatching train offering a high degree of passenger comfort was necessary. The first manifestations of this attitude appeared with the new Class 319 Thameslink stock from York in 1987, and the Class 442 Bournemouth stock from BREL Derby in 1988, both of which are dealt with in Part 10 of this series. Thus the appearance of the first Class 321 EMU from BREL York was eagerly awaited, and enthusiasts were not to be disappointed.

The front end profile follows that of the Class 442, but the absence of conventional drawgear enables the lower part to be made very neat indeed, with the Tightlock coupler and connection block protruding from the streamlined cowling, which has slightly less rake. Perhaps the most surprising feature, to the writer at least, is the absence of the wrap-around windscreen design which had reappeared on the Class 442 and which, in the knowledge that neither gangway connections nor an end door would be provided on the Class 321, was thought to be a racing certainty!

Another innovation, first seen on the Class 442, is a dot-matrix destination indicator which is set by the driver from a calculator-type keyboard. Unfortunately the visibility of this feature from any distance, particularly in bright sunshine, leaves something to be desired.

I have already mentioned the need to eliminate the 'waste' of floor space immediately behind the driving compartment, where a cross vestibule has been provided for the use of the traincrew. The elimination of this feature to the satisfaction of all concerned had taxed the ingenuity of design staff for some time and a number of unsatisfactory solutions had been developed. Experience with Class 141 and 142 DMMU trains for example, where the driver has to pass through a possibly crowded public area to open the passenger doors to alight and use a lineside telephone, demonstrated that arrangement to be unsatisfactory. The Class 151

prototype DMMU trains built by Metro-Cammell, and now alas withdrawn, showed what could be done. With these units the driving compartment had its own exterior sliding door, albeit requiring a 'pocket' into which it had to slide upon opening. The Class 321 driving compartment therefore has a sliding plug door which rests neatly alongside the bodyside when open and remains in gauge, something that could not be said of the outwards-opening slam doors that were fitted to several earlier DMMU classes. Providing the power-operated door does not inadvertently open when the driver or guard has his head out of the window, and

t remains draught-free, then it would appear that the ideal solution has at last been found.

The Class 321 production line is destined to be a long one as Network SouthEast's November 1988 *New Train Build Time-able*, expressed in numbers of vehicles, shows although at that time not all of the 1989/90 build and none of that for 1990/91 had been authorised:

1988/89	1989/90	1990/91
136	168	100

The build of units for the LMR Northampton services, following the completion of unit No 346, incorporates an additional nine first class seats and forms a sub-class numbered 321401 onwards. Orders for Classes 321/3 and 321/4 were placed in the autumn of 1989.

Details of Class 321: Built York 1988/89

DTS	19.95×2.82m	29.06t		78S	T3-7 bogies
MS	19.92×2.82m	51.51t		81S	P7-4 bogies
ATS	19.92×2.82m	28.80t		76S	T3-7 bogies
DTC	19.95×2,82m	29,31t	19F	58S	T3-7 bogies

Sets numbered 321301-321376

DTS	numbered	78049-78094
MS	numbered	62975-63020*
TS	numbered	71880-71925
DTC	numbered	77853-77898

*MS has four Brush TM2141B 268kW motors and pantograph

Below:
Class 321 unit No 321337 leaves Broxbourne with a Cambridge to Liverpool Street service on 17 June 1989, with DTC vehicle No 78085 leading. Already the paintwork above the driving compartment windows appears to be deteriorating. *Alec Swain*

Bottom:
Having stopped a discreet distance from the buffer stops (the absence of conventional buffers decrees such caution!) DTS vehicle No 77861 shows the 'P' suffix to the unit number, 321309, which indicates to GPO and platform staff that the parcels accommodation is in that vehicle. When it is required for use, usually on specifically designated services, the adjacent double-leaf door controls are no longer passenger controlled and an illuminated sign adjacent to the 'door open' button displays the wording 'Door not in use'. *Alec Swain*

Right:

The unique power-operated sliding plug door to the driving compartment of a Class 321 unit, which does not require a 'pocket' in the bodyside to accommodate it when in the open position. *Alec Swain*

Below right:

For driver training and staff familiarisation purposes, two Class 321 units were loaned to the LMR prior to that Region receiving its own units numbered from 347 onwards. However, a Gala Day at Northampton on 13 May 1989 found unit No 321321 in public service operating a special shuttle service to Rugby, at a fare of 20p (child 10p) return! *Alec Swain*

Below:

The other Class 321 unit on loan to the LMR, No 321320, is stabled in the centre sidings at the south end of Rugby station on 24 June 1989. The DTS vehicle, No 77872, is nearest the camera. *Alec Swain*

A Look at the Future

The next new classes of overhead line EMU trains to appear from BREL York will be Class 320 for Strathclyde PTA, followed by Class 322 for Liverpool Street to Stansted Airport services, both due for introduction during the 1990/91 financial year. Although based on the Class 321 units, different formations and internal arrangements merit the allocation of separate class designations. Brief details are already available and are listed below:

18 Class 320 BREL York, ScR Services

Introduced: 1990
Purpose: To replace the remaining unrefurbished ScR Class 303 units and all Class 311
No of cars per unit: Three
Unit numbers: 320301-320322
Vehicle numbers: DTS numbered 77899-77942 T3-7 bogies
MS numbered 63021-63042* P7-4 bogies
PMS has four Brush TM2141B 249kW motors

Right:
Artist's impression of the forthcoming Class 320 design for Strathclyde services.
BREL

19 BREL York, Stansted Airport Services Class 322

Introduced: 1990/91
Purpose: Liverpool Street to Stansted Airport services
No of cars per unit: Four
Unit numbers: 322481-322485
Vehicle numbers: To be announced. DTS, DTC and TS vehicles all with T3-7 bogies; PMS vehicles with P7-4 bogies. PMS has four Brush TM2141B 249kW motors.

The Class 322 units will carry a special 'airport' livery and will be finished internally to a higher standard, eg they will be carpeted throughout and floor-to-ceiling luggage stacks will be provided.

It is then likely that some 30 Class 323 three-car units will be built for Provincial sector for use in Birmingham and in the Network NorthWest area as replacements for the 1960-built Class 304 units. In Birmingham, the 'cross-city' Lichfield to Redditch service could then be a likely candidate for electrification.

Future construction will depend upon the need to replace the early units, and progress with further electrification schemes, in particular the plans to link existing London suburban routes by two Crossrail tunnels and, in Manchester, a new light rapid transport system to be known as Metrolink. This latter scheme will involve the laying of tramway-type tracks through Manchester city centre to connect the Bury and Altrincham routes, which will be converted to light rail operation, no doubt in a similar manner to the Docklands Light Railway in London. The new trains to be built for this system will effectively replace the unique Class 504 dc third rail units and any remaining Class 304 units. The next step would surely be to extend this Metrolink system to the Glossop/Hadfield and Wilmslow via East Didsbury routes thereby lessening still further the need to build replacement main line EMU trains. We shall see!

So far as the London area is concerned, it is likely to be the late 1990s before services such as Shenfield to Reading could be introduced, via the projected Crossrail tunnels under London, but this would at last bring electrification to the WR's suburban services and would link up with the Paddington to Heathrow service which is still planned for 1992/93.

Whilst Class 321 and its derivatives will meet the short-term requirement for new trains, the next generation of overhead line EMU trains is already being developed and this is liable to have far-reaching consequences for future electrification schemes. Readers will be aware of the experimental four-car Class 457 unit that has operated on the SR third rail system, formed mainly of Class 210 DEMU vehicles (see *BR Fleet Survey 9*) as a testbed for the Class 465 'Networker' dc third rail units. The significance of this is that Brush 165kW three phase *ac* traction motors are fitted to the DMS vehicles, Nos 67300 and 67301. This has been the dream of many an electric traction engineer in past years as there are considerable savings to be had from such a system, but it is only very recently that technology has finally provided the means to adapt ac motors for rail traction purposes. These two vehicles have subsequently been formed into a four-car

Above:
The livery for the forthcoming Class 322 'Stansted Express' was demonstrated on a Class 321 DTC at BREL York on 3 July 1989.
Barry J. Nicolle

Right:
The Networker 2 prototype, numbered 316999, at Colchester depot on 7 November 1989, prior to starting test running in the Colchester area. *Michael J. Collins*

formation including a TS vehicle from a Class 313 unit; thus the pantograph of the latter can collect current to be fed, via jumper cables, to the ac traction motors of the DMS vehicles. This experimental unit, numbered 316999, began trial running on the Colchester to Clacton line during November 1989. However, a production build of such units, likely to materialise as Class 331 for the Fenchurch Street services, would have another feature — regenerative braking. This allows for the current that is produced during rheostatic braking (as available on Classes 314 and 315) to be fed back into the overhead line, and hence into the CEGB National Grid. It is estimated that there will be 30% energy savings as a result which will surely have a marked effect on the costing of any future schemes. Once again, we shall see.